RIDING IT OUT

To Colin + Mary

Best wishes

Riding It Out

Pam.

Pam Goodall

UPFRONT PUBLISHING
LEICESTERSHIRE

Riding It Out
Copyright © Pam Goodall 2004

ISBN 1-84426-310-X

First published 2004 by
UPFRONT PUBLISHING LTD
Leicestershire

Printed by CopyTECH (UK) Limited

Acknowledgements

*Linda Cox – whose enthusiasm and informative flow of
every aspect of cycling led me to discover that such a
journey is possible. Her constant support before, during
and since has been invaluable.*

*Diana Biggs – who undertook more than I because she
organised my life during my absence. Without her, my
journey would not have been possible and my filing has
never been in better shape.*

*Ian Hutchinson – who facilitated contacts throughout the
company which ensured that my vagabond status was
memorably transformed to that of VIP on several
occasions.*

*Sue Greene – who did everything short of starting her
own newspaper or magazine in her efforts to secure a
media outlet to cover the journey.*

*The CTC – who supplied invaluable information
collated from members, all for the price of the postage,
which helped formulate ideas about the route and
inspired the idea of following the Danube.*

To
Russell and Gavin
with love

'Until you are committed, there is
hesitancy, a chance to draw back,
ineffectiveness.
At the moment you definitely commit
yourself, providence moves too.
All sorts of things occur to help that which
would never otherwise have
happened.
A whole stream of events, all manner of
unforeseen incidents and meetings.
Whatever you can do, or dream, begin it.
Boldness has genius, power, magic. Begin
it now.'

Goethe

EUROPE

Chapter One

It is shortly after dawn on a perfect spring morning. The sun is low in a cloudless pale blue sky and the calm waters of the English Channel reflect this mood. I am standing at the head of a lengthening queue of cars waiting to board the ferry. This is not because I arrived first, but because I arrived on a bicycle. Legitimate queue barging without repercussions. No raised fist or honking horn, not even a glare. Just a few curious glances. Clutched in my hand the £5 ferry ticket, foot passenger day return, does not reflect the truth. I will not be returning but a single fare costing £25 is more expensive. Even with the bicycle travelling free of charge, it had been too tempting not to take the risk. But I feel anxious about its validity, aware that the four bulging panniers clipped to the front and back of the bike might arouse suspicion. Just how much luggage does one need for a day in France?

'Morning, luv' says one of the group of men in charge of loading. He releases the barrier and invites me to proceed, holding the cars back until I have safely bumped my heavy bike up the ramp. 'Take it easy' he encourages me 'and tuck the bike away down this side. Make sure you lock it up. You can't trust anybody these days.'

'Thanks' I reply, my grin challenging the width of the distant watery horizon.

Upstairs in the restaurant I am absorbed with the first of three Michelin maps which are to guide me eastwards through France, when a man approaches.

'Do you have a corkscrew?' An unusual request from a stranger at six o'clock in the morning. And why me? The temptation is to say no, because the Swiss army knife buried amongst other tools is tightly packed as I haven't planned on needing it this early in the journey. But if he and his friends fancy a glass of wine, who am I to deny it?

'I saw you arriving at the terminal on a bike' he says. 'Looks as if you're expecting to be away for a while.' Could he be an undercover ticket inspector?

'I'm cycling around the world' I tell him, words that still cause a tingle to run up my spine.

'Are you meeting up with a friend in Calais?'

'Oh no, I'm travelling by myself.'

'What – by yourself? Good heavens. That's absolutely amazing. What a prospect. I really envy you; it's something that I'd love to do.' His eyes widen and he goes on to tell me about his experiences over-landing from New Zealand to the UK. In return for the corkscrew, he passes on several travel tips (in the absence of a single Lonely Planet guide any advice from a seasoned traveller will be appreciated and absorbed) and then returns to his group.

As the ferry approaches Calais an hour later he makes a point of coming over to me again. 'I wanted to wish you the best of luck and hope you have a safe journey' he says shaking me very firmly by the hand.

This gesture comes to symbolise how people will react to the presence of me and my bicycle during the coming months. Curious and kind (but fortunately never again needing to borrow anything).

Awaiting disembarkation, my high level of energy and alertness do not reflect the sleepless night endured at the Dover Youth Hostel. This was at the end of the second day of my journey and the enormity of the decision was taking hold. Insuppressible anxieties overwhelmed physical exhaustion and so the night had dragged on as I lay wide awake on the lower bunk of a crowded dormitory, checking my watch all too frequently and listening to the untroubled breathing of others. It had been a relief to get up at five o'clock.

Now the challenge is to find my way out of the terminal and through the streets of Calais and it is proving frustrating and dangerous because signposts are intended for vehicles and lead towards categories of roads forbidden to cyclists. It is not made easier when some teenage boys sabotage my efforts by deliberately directing me the wrong way and laughing with sadistic satisfaction. This is an early clue that throughout the entire journey, cycling through twenty countries, it is only this category of individuals would feel the need to taunt and jeer.

The combination of one way streets, misleading signposts and false directions are sapping my buoyant mood and the return half of that ticket is lurking in my luggage – intended as a souvenir.... Then success – lush green fields, acres of uninterrupted countryside, an inviting open road and no traffic – the confusion of Calais is in my wake. Just how good is it possible to feel? I cannot resist the urge to let out a yelp of delight, tempered with relief.

This is the first of many firsts. Other than the need to cycle to work or the shops, all previous trips on a bike have been as part of a group. Whether a Sunday ride to a pub, a weekend on the Isle of Wight or the thrills of mountain biking in Nepal, I have never been on my own. With navigation the responsibility of someone else, the only demand on me was not to lose sight of the bum in front, irrespective of shape or size and no matter how bright the lycra.

A mistaken turning can involve an energy sapping, time consuming and demoralising detour. The ability to interpret a road map is critical. An hour's drive in a car – say sixty miles – is a day's ride on a bicycle and the very last thing you want to discover is that you've cycled ten miles in the wrong direction.

The temperature is 35°C and it seems advisable to break out with the Factor 15. This particular item of luggage is buried deep in the large pannier because it's intended to offer protection from the sun while travelling through Iran and this is my first day in France. Even so, no sun block can prevent that ludicrous cyclist tan. My daily apparel of baggy shorts and T-shirt, baseball cap and sandals create an unflattering unfinished jigsaw look, the most bizarre give-away being the tell-tale smudge of brown on the back of each hand from the Velcro fastening of the cut-off mittens. Sunbathing in a bikini will definitely be out of the question.

But then a bikini is not part of my luggage. Like many other items, it had been left behind. Before setting off, radical decisions were made as to what to take. All original thoughts of a jumbo tube of toothpaste, large shower gel, hairbrush, six T-shirts, a pair of jeans, sweat shirt, spare bottle of moisturiser had to be abandoned. And the packing itself was very precise. After many trials, I discovered that, depending on sequence and method, the identical amount of gear could either take up about three quarters of the space available or, with panniers overflowing, the bulk of essentials would still be sitting on the bed.

It's now Tuesday. Could it really only be last Sunday that all the planning ended and my family and friends gathered to say goodbye? After group photographs and emotional hugs, I set off unsteadily down a steep driveway with a wave and a wobble. Such ignominy to have fallen off before even reaching the road. The full impact of my solo journey was cushioned that first day by the presence of Linda, who had suggested accompanying me and even carried one of the large panniers – the gesture of a true friend. As we meandered along the quiet country lanes of West Sussex we were blessed with perfect cycling conditions (which means above all else no head wind) and surrounded by all the evidence of Spring.

The problems started in the late afternoon when Linda headed for the train and my search for a bed and breakfast began. Before leaving I had shrugged off the many suggestions to pre-book the first night – *'for peace of mind'*. But no, stubborn and idealistic, I argued that this was not in the spirit of the undertaking and in any case would never be an option once over the Channel. It smacked of cheating. And anyway, even if I cycled further than the Sussex county border, the people in Kent speak English don't they? How difficult could it be?

I was about to find out.

The village shop was still open. 'I'm sorry to bother you, but please could you tell me where I'll find the nearest B&B?'

'That's very easy' replied the woman at the till. 'The pub down the end of the road has rooms. It's on the left. You can't miss it.'

As a precaution I added 'Is that the only one or do you know of any others?' At this point a couple of locals joined in and after a short discussion they gave the names of four more, together with directions. Confident and elated, but by now feeling the effects of the sixty miles which we had covered since leaving, I cycled the last few hundred yards to be told that the pub was fully booked. Relieved in a way – pubs can be noisy and my sole intention was a very hot bath and a very early night – there were four others to choose from. No problem….

This exercise of finding the first night's accommodation wouldn't be worthy of comment had it been tackled in a car. At the very worst, it might have seemed an irritation. It is also not enough to relate that it took another two hours, a further twenty miles of pedalling and near total collapse.

To get to the first place meant retracing five of the miles that Linda and I had just cycled, in itself deeply demoralising, to find the promised signpost 'B&B $1^1/_4$ miles'. This gave no clue, however, of the private drive, a leg draining extra mile of pot holes plummeting downhill. Fantasies of hot tea and hot bath were immediately dashed when a grumpy, spotty youth responded to my knock.

'I've followed the signs for your B&B and would like to have a bed for the night.'

'My mum's out and my dad's not around' he told me, ready to shut the door.

'Hang on a minute. When will they be back?' The thought of retracing tracks up that steep, bone crunching, energy sapping drive was unthinkable.

'Not sure. And anyway, I don't think she's doing B&B anymore.' And that was it. He shut the door, leaving me no choice but to head back up the vertical drive. Hadn't anybody thought about taking the wretched sign down?

My worst nightmare, even before leaving, was the thought of not having found somewhere to stay before dark. Somehow the idea of cycling around at night, with no idea of where I would be sleeping, was very frightening. But, the way I felt just then was far more menacing. It was not the fear of day light running out but of my energy seeping away. I was feeling very, very tired.

The search didn't end at either of the next two places. Several miles and hills later, only to find the first house was deserted – no reply after nearly beating the door down – and from the second 'Sorry dear, it's too early in the season. We won't be opening for another month.'

Overcome with rage and disbelief and trying not to panic, there was one more name on the list and amidst the puffing and panting, there was this chastising, nagging voice in my head reminding me of all those conversations advising me to be sensible and pre-book. Just as the 'sleeping under a hedge' option was becoming all too real, rescue came from a man unloading a truck in his drive. Sensing my desperation he phoned the B&B which was owned by a woman he knew well. My plight had not been helped with dyslexic directions confusing 'fork left' for 'fork right' and I was not going to budge from his gateway until he had described every bend, rise, hedge, tree, gate, style, footpath, pylon, telegraph pole, cow and birds nest along the route.

It worked. Gill was waiting in the evening sun to welcome me. Living in an idyllic cottage with a garden full of blossom and bird song, and an assortment of bantams and pigs roaming amongst the flower beds, she was fascinated to hear my story. The details were gradually revealed over a steaming mug of tea and half the contents of the sugar bowl. (I haven't drunk tea with sugar since I was a kid but my body was giving out strong messages that could not be ignored.) Then, with barely the energy to climb the stairs, I collapsed into an equally steaming bath and enjoyed my last fix of '*Have I Got News For You*'.

Next morning Gill would not hear of taking any money for my night's stay. 'I am so thrilled to be part of your journey' she said over breakfast 'and even more so because it is the very first night. I insist that you should be my guest.' My protests were futile. I felt embarrassed, but she was adamant. This too was a sign of things to come.

Never had I imagined that the end of the first day would result in feeling so utterly exhausted and exasperated. Was this a serious flavour of what lay ahead? Oh how I hoped not. But there were lessons to be learned; not least that without two litres of internal combustion engine under a bonnet, detours to all points of the compass at the end of a long day's ride were something to be avoided. The tent, which had only been packed on a 'just in case' basis, very nearly made an early appearance. Whether or not I would have had the strength to put it up was debatable.

There is a small postscript to the first day. The bicycle's bell didn't make it. It had fallen off unnoticed. Attached to the handlebars with Asia in mind (some idea of making The Team's presence felt amongst all those crowds) it hadn't survived twenty four hours, never mind let out a single warning ring. It had to be hoped that Chas Roberts had done a better job with the rest of the bicycle. There I was setting off around the world on a bespoke and expensive machine and the bell hadn't survived five miles.

Chapter Two

The destination this evening is a campsite marked on the map at the limit of my distance for the day. On arrival, it is closed. *'Fermé'* is the bleak message on a padlocked gate. The torment of my first night's search is still all too vivid. Having learnt nothing, I meekly turn away in search of what.... I am not entirely sure.

A *'so-what'* attitude or common sense should have prevailed. Pitch the tent at the campsite. Nobody would object – there was nobody there. Instead, an enquiry at the town hall results in the mayor's office grinding into action. What is it about the French? They certainly don't need lessons in bloody mindedness, especially when they can smell an English wind-up. As much as my body might welcome the unscheduled rest, ten minutes is wasted on the phone confirming that the site is indeed closed, with an added somewhat smug observation that, even if it were open, they would have turned me away – it only caters for caravans. A second lengthy phone call establishes that there is another campsite only fourteen kilometres away. *'Only'* maybe in the mayor's Peugeot, but far from *'only'* when viewed from my saddle.

'In that case I would much prefer to stay in the town and pay for a gîte. I really don't have the energy to cycle any further.' This seems a justified extravagance with both legs and bum feeling the effects of three extremely untypical days of cycling.

'I am sorry, Madame, there are none in the town. But do not worry, it is not a problem. They are expecting you at the campsite and it only takes ten minutes to get there.'

'Not if you're on a bicycle' I mutter as sarcastically as my rusty French will allow.

Having covered sixty miles already, the ordeal of the next hour's ride is compounded by the fact that I have only eaten fruit during the day. The woman at the till of a small village shop failed to see the funny side when presented with a banana skin amongst the other purchases of apples and oranges. In my haste to top up my tumbling blood sugar level, it completely escaped my mind that all fruit had to be weighed. As juicy, sweet and refreshing as fruit might be, it doesn't scratch the surface of the need to replace the squillions of calories disappearing through the pedals. My legs feel empty and it is only sheer will power that is keeping me going. The last two kilometres seem like two hundred and two miles. I am very weak, too weak even to feel upset or angry. The gradient is brutal and I am forced to stop intermittently to allow what strength is left to seep back into my wobbly legs. When I finally arrive an hour after leaving the mayor's office, I am on the verge of collapse and the site is deserted. The promised welcome has given up and gone home. Did anyone bother to mention that I am on a bicycle?

There is some flat ground about fifty yards from Reception where I intend to pitch the tent. By now unable even to push the loaded Alchemy, I unclip the panniers and stagger back and forth carrying them one at a time. After locking the bicycle to a tree, the urgent need to lie down has to be ignored in the presence of very black threatening clouds approaching at speed, judging by the sound of a wind that is blasting through the trees.

(Alchemy is the name I've chosen for the bicycle. 'It's only a tool' observed Chas Roberts. That's as maybe, but it is also a vital companion without which no mile, tortuous or otherwise, would be covered. It had been important that the name was genderless and the connotations of *'progress'* and *'development'* were ones which I hoped would become symbolic of the journey.)

The modern tent is a superb example of technology and design. Long gone are the days when it takes three people to erect a two-man tent. No squat fat tent pegs inclined to leave splinters; no guy ropes to trip the unwary or slacken mysteriously in the night; no seeping heavy canvas; no poles lurching at an angle and impossible to avoid when asleep. What I had not bargained for during rehearsals on a saturated lawn was pitching my one-person refuge on grass with all the characteristics of marble. The pegs (more accurately resembling skewers because they are perfectly designed for kebabs on a barbecue) prove incapable of penetrating even one centimetre of the solid ground, never mind the depth needed to secure the tent. And there are six of them. The problem is made no easier in the absence of a hammer. At no point when deciding what to take on this journey had a hammer made it onto the most optimistic and lengthy list. Even without other campers from whom it should be possible to borrow, there would surely always be a decent rock in the vicinity. (Back in Sussex it had been possible to push these pegs in with my thumb!)

Ignoring all temptations to become hysterical and allow questions of *just what on earth am I doing here?'* to surface, I go in search of the rock. Even a decent stone would be up to the job, but there is nothing. It is as if the ground has been swept, so I have to settle by improvising with a handful of crumbling pebbles, pouring water from the bicycle bottles in a futile effort to soften the ground. The final grain of patience, will power and energy evaporate as I collapse inside onto my bed mat, close the zip and two minutes later the promised storm erupts. Spectacular thunder and lightening directly overhead and rain which redefines torrential. Having spent my childhood in South Africa I had never failed to be thrilled by such storms, tucked up in the safety of my bed alert to the sights, sounds and smells. But nothing has prepared me for the stupefying drama of being in a tiny fragile tent. The expectation that it too could collapse any minute adds a certain frisson.

There had been little, in fact no detailed planning of this journey. The idea is to travel east, ensuring the sun on my face in the morning and on my back in the evening, thus making the incomplete tan several shades darker on the right side than that on the left. About twenty countries were plotted on an atlas which left less to go wrong and more opportunity for spontaneity. The only aspect that was a dead cert was the need for food – troughs of it several times a day. Cakes and pastries would no longer be classified as a luxury but as essential fuel. Calories galore; restraint a thing of the past. I had been looking forward to it, saliva glands at the ready. Or so I thought. At a conscious level I could look anyone in the eye and say that I was not only feeling excited but also very confident about the venture. However, deep down there must have been anxiety and nightmare of nightmares, this was choosing to manifest itself in lack of appetite. My stomach was in reject mode, refusing to join The Team and this resulted in an overwhelming feeling of nausea at the smell and sight of food. How cruel is that? On the first day the pub lunch and teatime cakes with Linda were a struggle, when normally every last crumb would have been hoovered down with delight and appreciation. The much anticipated full English breakfast presented proudly by Gill was picked at and swallowed with enormous difficulty. Even the croissants on the ferry had to be washed down with coffee. Force feeding was proving no fun.

Lying all but comatose in my sleeping bag there are worrying danger signs. My calves and feet are seized with convulsing cramps. Somewhere in the depths of a pannier are salt tablets, but my exhaustion ensures they remain untouched. They too were intended for Iran.

A couple of days later the sight of a mobile friterie doing business on the side of the road seems the perfect way to coax my appetite back. Chips without guilt and with plenty of salt. Genuine French fries will surely prove irresistible – as turns out to be the case. My jubilation is not reflected by the man who serves me, obviously horrified as the contents of the salt shaker are dumped on his meticulously prepared *'pommes frites'*. He flinches and turns away and sadly my French is inadequate when it comes to an explanation.

By the end of the first week I have eaten one proper traditional meal. This was at an auberge in the evening. My least favourite pastime is to sit by myself in a busy restaurant but it was the next attempt to persuade the stroppy stomach to stop sulking. The choice of food had been unimportant – all that mattered was that the salt cellar was full.

All pre-conceptions about availability and cheapness of gîtes are destroyed, but I do treat myself a couple of times. The luxury of a bed (especially a pillow – the only home comfort that I am missing) and endless hot water in the bath or shower justify the extravagance. It also enables me to do some washing and enjoy the only benefit of the unseasonal heat because the dripping clothes dry within an hour. On both these gîte stops, the Madame joined me for an early breakfast. The first one spent the entire meal complaining about her Swedish neighbours and the ants getting into the jam, and the second ate all the bread which had been reheated from the previous day – surely a criminal offence in France. Perhaps eating solo has its advantages.

During this first week there is another perfectly planned arrival at the town where a campsite is clearly marked on the map and particularly comforting, a sign several kilometres back down the road confirming its existence. Only to find (would I never learn) it's bloody *fermé*. It is beginning to feel like a conspiracy. There is a gîte but it is full and the Hotel Commercial is disgusting and way beyond my budget. Undaunted, *'Plan B'* is adopted. There are legendary stories about cyclists (usually impoverished male students) knocking on the door of a private home requesting permission to pitch the tent in the owner's garden. This not only offers diverse options for accommodation (no more cycling for two hours) but also cuts down dramatically on costs. Necessity might be the mother of invention, but it is also the first cousin of courage. A week ago it would have been unimaginable that I could have contemplated approaching the home of complete stranger (never mind a French stranger) to seek some form of refuge.

Sooner than expected the town is behind me, no suitable home having been spotted. Anticipating a scattering of farms I continue but become alarmingly aware during the next hour that this road is a major feeder route into Luxembourg. Instinct lures me down a country lane to the front door of a miniature castle. Even in the grey mist and damp of the early evening it is impressive, standing in a large walled and wooded garden. While knocking I wonder what the French for 'knackered' is. The man who opens the door understands immediately my stuttering attempt to make this unusual request, my body language perhaps compensating for my lack of verbal fluency. He takes it so much in his stride one could almost believe it was a regular occurrence. After inviting me inside, he proudly treats me to an English cup of tea, shows me up to the shower and puts my sodden gear in the tumble drier. Sodden this time not as a result of gallons of sweat erupting from every pore, but from constant rain during the afternoon – the first on the trip and strangely welcome after unrelenting sunshine. It was only this wet and smelly state that prevented me from enveloping him with a hug of relief and gratitude on the doorstep. The family ask me to join them for supper but a picnic in the tranquil surroundings of the garden seems preferable. Today eighty five (and a half) miles have been ridden much to my astonishment – an even more impressive one hundred and thirty seven kilometres.

Chapter Three

Finding somewhere to stop each night is turning out to be anything but a formality. It is the only truly significant difference to normal life. In the world that most of us are familiar with, nothing is more certain than that we know each day where we will be sleeping that night. To take this out of the equation is something that it is impossible to prepare for. Being aware in no way cushions the reality. There is a real danger that all thoughts during the daytime cycling hours are becoming consumed with where I will be sleeping that night – a level of anxiety that is unacceptable. It is essential to trick my thoughts from falling into this Catch 22 trap. Worrying isn't going to solve the problem and destroys the *'being there'* sense of wonder. And as nothing is going to change, the sooner these anxious thoughts are not just pushed to one side but dispensed with altogether, the more the ride each day will be appreciated. A sound theory, but how easy would it be to put into practice?

There is another battle going on, this time not mind games but physical in the most basic sense. It is between the Brooks saddle and my bum. The odds-on favourite to win is the saddle. Brooks is to saddles what Rolls Royce is to cars. Perceived to be the absolute best and recognised all over the world. Passers-by might not speak a word of English but they recognise the Brooks saddle. Judging from its appearance, nothing seems to have changed since the original prototype. There is nothing bottom-friendly about the materials it is made from. No hi-tech soft modern fabrics; no hint of soothing squidgy gel or shock absorbing springs. But it is extremely elegant, made from leather (very, very hard leather) held in place with metal studs (very, very hard metal studs). Come to think of it, the perfect alternate hammer. Back in

Croydon Chas Roberts' assuring words were 'Once the saddle has eventually been broken in, you become quite unaware of it after a day's cycling'. Humph. Suffice to say that at this point my bum is only too painfully aware of the saddle and extremely concerned to know just how long *'eventually'* might be.

Diana, my invaluable anchor back in England, has extracted a promise that emails would arrive as frequently as is sensibly possible. There was no way of judging before setting off exactly what *'frequent'* meant and the last thing either of us wanted was for her to unleash an unnecessary and embarrassing search. The French have a word for a place where one might gain public access to the Internet. It is *'cyber café'*. But one has to question just why, as I never managed to find one. After extensive telephone research, the owner of a gîte divulged the fact that such a café was to be found seventy kilometres south. Even in a car this would be considered an excessive diversion, but on a bicycle.... Not even the image of Diana's hand hovering above the panic button could persuade me that this detour was an option.

Noticing a Tourist Information in the next major city, it seems sensible to pursue the Internet search by popping in and enquiring where I might find the *cyber café*. There will probably even be a choice. But *'popping in'* is more complicated when your entire home, four panniers and a bicycle, has to be left unattended outside. (This would be at the top of a short list of the advantages of travelling with a companion, as one could stand guard while the other does the business.) To prop the bicycle against a wall or tree without locking it would be foolhardy in the extreme. I had vowed before leaving that the temptation to do this would never happen, however short the errand was deemed to be. To return and find.... nothing.... journey's end, melt down. To ensure that this never occurred, or at least make the job of the thief extremely troublesome, I had invested in two identical locks, each which stretched to six feet. This made it possible to secure the bicycle to anything from a narrow rail to a huge tree trunk with one lock, and to lead the other one through the frame and then the handles of three of the panniers. (The fourth never leaves my side, containing passport, cash and bank card.) It is a time-consuming process with no short cuts.

Having gone through all this paraphernalia, I join the queue inside. The predictable answer to *'Parlez vous Anglais?'* is a self satisfied *'Non'* from the menopausal cardigan-clad woman behind the glass. Switching to halting French (which has worked well enough so far) I ask if there is a *cyber café* in the town. Had I been speaking fluent double-Dutch or treble-Swahili the reaction could not be more blank and uncomprehending. Determined not to be intimidated, words keep tumbling out about cycling alone through France and wanting to communicate with family and friends back in England who are expecting to hear from me. Even her non-verbal communications convey a clear message – the irritated shrug of her shoulders comes over as offensive and unwelcoming. The discussion is brought to an abrupt end when she points aggressively towards the exit sniping something in French about *'postcards and stamps'* and followed by 'Next....'

Email success is in my grasp in St Die, but the French system wins again. Following instructions which result in ricocheting between the tourist office, the mayor's office, the students headquarters and a computer shop, it becomes clear that the purchase of a ticket would buy me an hour on the Internet. Flushed with a feeling of triumph and clutching the expensive *billet*, I return to the computer shop – to find it has closed for a two hour lunch. Needing food myself, I buy a huge vegetarian baguette but, not realising that part of the filling would be *pommes frites*, I have ordered a portion of *pommes frites* as well. This is another first – a chip butty with chips on the side. Oh well, at least I should have a positive calorie balance for the day. When the Internet shop eventually opens, the confusion of the different layout of the keyboard nullifies all my touch typing skills and as a class of school kids are pre-booked, I am slung out after twenty minutes. My protests, in whatever language, are in vain and with no time to check through what I have written, my email message would bear all the evidence of being encrypted.

An invitation from Diana's sister gives me an excuse to loop north to Luxembourg. The detour brings its own rewards – the unimaginable thrill of arriving at a capital city, albeit a small one, on a bicycle and the opportunity to become a complete slob for two days. I resist all offers to sightsee, preferring instead to eat sufficient to satisfy a pregnant with triplets sumo wrestler – a celebratory end to involuntary anorexia – while my salty cycling gear experiences the joys of a washing machine. It is becoming clear, however, that with the soaring temperatures no matter how effectively the daily sweat and odours are removed from my body and clothes, the fragrant freshness vanishes within half an hour of starting out the next morning.

A focal point of the route in Europe is to join the Danube and follow it through Germany, Austria, Slovakia and Hungary which will give me a double advantage: minimal navigation and a dedicated cycle route (no hills hee hee). But first I have to get there which means crossing the Black Mountains.

It is this day which brings the first real cycling, well to be more accurate, pushing challenge. The combination of my insistence in avoiding main roads, together with the confusion of a German contour map specially produced for cyclists, finds me struggling up steep rocky tracks through the forest. A bike is for riding. It is wheelbarrows which are designed to be pushed. But even a wheelbarrow would prove difficult if the load weighed more than the person pushing and the gradient was a bumpy 1:4. As I discover, if you can't ride a bike up a hill, then pushing it is not an easy option – in fact it is absolute hell. And the knowledge that I am lost compounds my misery. After a couple of hours of stumbling tearful exhaustion, I emerge on to an otherwise deserted road to find Daniel, a twenty two year old German on a touring bike. He is cycling down to the South of France to join friends for the summer and is enjoying a picnic of cider, bread and cheese which he invites me to share. My recent ordeal is quickly forgotten as we swap stories and his parting words to me are 'Have a safe journey and no flat tyres....'

And so it happens, one hundred yards later, my first puncture. Now, punctures are to cycling what barbecues are to cooking: men's work. That's the unwritten rule. So, although I have had several punctures over the years, I have never fixed one, because I have always been part of a group. A fact that, when setting off on a bike ride around the world, would seem to denote an extreme form of insanity. So, testing the my explanation and theory of *'there's always been a man around'* to the limit, I swiftly return to catch Daniel packing up. He cheerfully fulfils his role of knight on a shining bike and appreciates the irony of the circumstances. Even the most sceptical could not deny the synchronicity – we are in the middle of nowhere; not a single car has passed during our hour's encounter; we are the only people for miles. And even more remarkable, he is not just any man, he is an accomplished cyclist well practised in the art of puncture repair.

The myth is that France loves cyclists, but the reality is different. What they love is the Tour de France and the only cyclists are lycra clad males with wrap around sunglasses on racing bikes with wheels skinnier than a centime. In Germany things are different. Everybody cycles wearing everyday clothes, whether it is to work, to the shops, to school or just out for a ride with a friend. As a result the cycling facilities are superb and very safe, whether in towns or in the country. Many roads have an entirely separate cycle track running parallel, thus sparing the unnerving experience of being smacked by the blast of air from a huge passing truck. At cross roads, men in BMWs cheerfully stop and wave me by, even if they have the right of way.

Whereas in France I was generally ignored, in Germany everyone wants to talk to me and if possible help. It is mid afternoon on a Sunday and once again my plan to camp is thwarted by a grumpy young receptionist. It is a combined '*gasthof*' and campsite and she has insisted that both are closed. I am determined to be assertive but my pleas for just a couple of square metres of grass are ignored as she continues to read her magazine.

'There is no water' she snarls.

I am working on a sharp retort in German of 'Who the bloody hell cares, I just want to lie down' when right on cue Peter and Uschi arrive on their bikes, out for their normal weekend ride. After telling my story, I find myself following them back to their home in Ehingen to stay the night.

Spontaneous kindness.

And there are plenty of examples: a very old gentleman in a town cycling miles out of his way to ensure I am on the right road (I hoped he would live long enough to make the return trip); a shopkeeper insisting on giving me an early morning coffee with the promise of a refill, while I browse through the maps on sale and she watches Alchemy (to save all that locking up routine); two women in a bakers phoning around the town to check on availability and prices of a hotel; a passer-by at a bus stop handing me a tissue to clean my hands which are covered in grease after fixing the chain which had come off, as well as a spare tissue in case it should happen again. (Ironically, I had grabbed a couple of leaves from a nearby tree in a futile effort to clean my fingers and I was sure that she was coming over to give me a bollocking for vandalising the tree.) Plus many, many more.

The balance of camping and using hotels is working well. Sleeping in a field alongside the Danube seemed to capture the spirit of adventure which was not only brought home by the isolation and lack of shower, but by deep guttural coughing just outside the tent. My pulse became supersonic as I tried to work out whether the sound could possibly be human. Had a torch shone through the canvas at that moment I would undoubtedly have died of fright. On the other hand, £12 at an inn not only provided endless hot water and a pillow, but also a huge breakfast of fresh rolls, several cheeses, jam, yoghurt and enough caffeine to jet propel me on to the agonising saddle.

The Danube proves to be a wonderful companion offering a diversity of landscape and wildlife. It is a powerful river and my picnic lunches sitting on its banks are never improved on during the coming months, whether watching swallows re-enacting scenes from The Dambusters or overladen barges struggling to make any headway against the fearsome current. The weirdest discovery is to see no sign of water sports – such activities as sailing, windsurfing, rowing, water-skiing. The fierce current deters any but the suicidal to enter its murky waters.

Chapter Four

Leaving Germany is a significant landmark for The Team. It had seemed so huge in the atlas back in Sussex. But the sense of achievement as I cycle into the fifth country of my journey is somewhat lessened by the lack of formal border crossing. The only indication when I entered Germany was the presence of a derelict customs house at the side of the road and the Mercedes or BMWs replacing the Renaults and Peugeots driving on it.

The need to plan the following day's route has brought about an addiction to map reading. But in Austria a map proves superfluous as the dedicated cycle route (the size of a country lane, the surface of a bowling green and not even a scooter allowed on its pristine tarmac) sticks absolutely to the banks of the river. In Germany it tended to stray off course through towns and cities, but the only choice to be made throughout Austria is whether to travel on the north or south bank. Bridges are infrequent but crossing is cheap and easy thanks to mini-ferries just for cyclists (such is the popularity of this route) which skim sideways to the other bank, dragged on a chain.

Vienna is the next major landmark where, thanks to my ex-boss, Ian Hutchinson and the wonders of email, I am expected at the offices of RSA. Even if dress-down had infiltrated this smart modern office, my cycling gear would be inappropriate, never mind that I have travelled fifty miles today in temperatures more suited to north Africa. Ian Sefton can barely conceal his horror as he welcomes me into his carpeted air conditioned office but to his eternal credit nevertheless invites me to stay a couple of days with him and Jane. They treat me to meals in smart restaurants where, dressed in crumpled trousers and T-shirt, I feel like orphan Annie. Jane recognises my anguish and as an agent for a range of clothing, dispatches me on my way with an outfit of long skirt, dressy T-shirt and a belt with gold beads – all black and miraculously uncrushable, a feature that is pushed to the limit during the coming months when it serves me magnificently at weddings, engagements, parties, dinners, barbecues.

The Danube leads me, very briefly, through Slovakia and this is the first experience of a border crossing with an up and running customs post. It all feels quite scary as for the first time I am entering into territory where the language is utterly strange to me and all those armed officers on duty look so fierce. There is a queue of trucks, coaches and cars stretching way back down the road and once again I have the immense satisfaction of unhesitatingly heading straight to the front of it. At times there are great advantages of not just being a cyclist, but also a middle aged woman, as everyone is happy to wave me through.

In the space of a few yards it is obvious that things have changed. A lamppost wobbles precariously as I lean the bicycle against it! On the outskirts of Bratislava I am asphyxiated by a black cloud of exhaust fumes belching out from the bus ahead – more pollution in these few seconds than in my entire life. The cycle track takes on the contours of a scramble course. In an effort to discourage motorbikes turning it into a race track, V-shaped knee high sleeping policemen have been built every fifty yards, interspersed with metal barriers barely wide enough to get the bike through. Having cycled over the first hump when the panniers were nearly ejected and I was all but sliced in half (sitting on that saddle was bad enough but having been propelled into the air and then landing heavily back on it....) dismounting becomes the only option.

In Hungary, the treasured cycle way evaporates and the Danube, which has been my constant companion for nearly a thousand miles, is glimpsed only occasionally until arriving in Budapest. My first night sets the tone of welcome and interest which I will encounter. A *'Zimmer Frei'* (room free) system operates throughout the country – the equivalent to B&B – at a cost of about £5.

With no clue where I might find one, I stop and ask in a small supermarket which is just about to close. The last customer tells me there is accommodation in the town but decides that any instructions would only cause confusion. Instead, she returns to the car where her husband and children are waiting and instructs him to drive slowly through the side streets so that I can follow them to the door.

Eva, a woman in her seventies, is working in her vegetable patch and she greets me with much touching and smiling and a huge jug of iced fresh lemon juice – such a joy when your thirst feels unquenchable and tepid water has been the only option all day. She then joins me in the garden where I am writing my diary and we are able to communicate in our various versions of German. Her cat takes a fancy to me and while I stroke it, I tell her that perhaps the cat could join The Team so that I would have someone to talk to during the long solitary hours in the saddle.

After supper of several delicious courses, I discover that she has arranged for a friend to give me an hour's massage, during which the masseuse discovers a tic on the back of my shoulder. This causes much screaming and consternation amongst the other three women (yes, there is an audience) where they seem inclined to abandon me and evacuate the room. Eva insists that I use all the family facilities, including her dressing gown and slippers, and sends me off to bed with a hot cocoa and pastry. In the meantime, Eva's Rumanian daughter-in-law has been in touch with her mother and furnished me with an invitation to stay with her relatives in the Rumanian mountains. In the morning the entire family are in the garden to see me on my way and attached to Alchemy's handlebars is a colourful knitted doll with an abundance of spiky black hair.

'Someone for you to talk to' says Eva.

I am not one for mascots, but Ellie (which the group agree should be her name) becomes part of the team.

Fuelled with a breakfast of three boiled eggs fresh from the chicken coop, fresh bread and salad, I head for the mountains anxious that, after one thousand miles of cuddling up to the flat banks of the Danube, any form of undulation will prove impossible. Will my legs, heart and lungs have all forgotten how to play their part? There are mountains ahead but with a kind gradient and a low granny gear progress is steady and painless. The road is quiet and the only vehicle to overtake is a luxury coach towing an enormous trailer. I reach the summit to find it parked up and a group of German cyclists are unloading their bicycles, ready for the downhill. This is definitely cycling for softies.

When all heads turn to greet me, I still have enough puff to punch the air and shout 'I did it the hard way' and am rewarded with beer and chocolate, accompanied inevitably by dozens of questions and a rather unexpected serenade on harmonica of *'Mull of Kintyre'*.

One of the older men looks directly at me and asks, without preamble, 'How old are you?'

Taken unawares, and not knowing the German for *'It's none of your business'* or *'Didn't your mother tell you that it is rude to ask women how old they are?'* I tell him 'Fifty eight' and it feels surprisingly good to do so. There isn't even the slightest temptation to deduct several years.

This is not my first introduction to the *'how old'* theme. It has been present from the beginning but is handled dramatically differently as I progress east. In Western Europe it might be asked, eventually and very obscurely, with a sense of embarrassment. Once I reach Hungary, and consistently from here on, it arises within the first three questions (the other two being *'what is your name?'* and *'where do you come from?'*) and is often the only question. This might sometimes be due to lack of English but by no means always. And if the only form of communication is sign language, it is still asked – and answered. If there is any doubt, the calculator is used to confirm the truth.

Linda has provided me with a contact just outside Budapest which is where I am headed.

As official sightseeing is not part of my agenda, I opt instead is to spend a couple of days cycling gently around Budapest where the greatest challenge is what flavour ice cream to choose. During my wanderings I fall into conversation with an American holding the hand of a six year old girl who speaks no English. It turns out that he and his wife are on a mission from Miami to adopt two children and have selected this girl and her baby sister. He tells me that they have been experiencing very disruptive behaviour from both children back at the hotel but he is confident all will settle quickly once they return to their newly set up home, complete with an abundance of cuddly toys. I suggest that their challenge will prove far more demanding than mine.

Csaba, my host, is horrified at my lack of culture en route. I have tried to explain to him that sightseeing and cycling are incompatible and if I had adopted his agenda, I would still be in France. He insists that I ought to visit cities and large towns to soak up the atmosphere. (As well as the fumes?) Intent at the very least on extending my local knowledge, he encourages me to visit a medieval town twenty miles north of Budapest which I do, only to find the place swarming with Japanese, Germans and Americans and every house in the centre has been converted into a souvenir shop or café. For me – a nightmare.

There is one unexpected bonus during the ride there. Situated between an eight lane highway, a hypermarket and a lake is a crowded nudist camp. All that covers the campers' vital statistics is either a hairy chest or stretch marks. There is nothing nubile or tasty here and my curiosity causes some unwelcome wobbling (their flesh and my bicycle). These bodies have been extravagantly lived in, experienced the good life to excess and are apparently proud of the evidence.

Fortunately (for inquisitive passers-by) the only form of recreation seems to be floating on a pedalo. To see everything jumping around a volley ball court would cause a multiple crash. There is even a trend amongst the Sunday cyclists to wear more on their head than the rest of their body.

Csaba has a big problem with my trip. Not only is he disgusted at my disinterest in museums, art galleries and cathedrals, he has also criticised the design of my bicycle and taken frightening pleasure in informing me of the extreme dangers in Rumania to say nothing of Bulgaria, which makes Rumania resemble Disneyland. As for Pakistan, one of his work colleagues left there because of the risks and appalling quality of life in the country. Then Vietnam: what about the land mines? He adds that he wouldn't want to do the trip – somewhat superfluously....

It is towards Lake Balaton that I am now pedalling. The name is unavoidable in a conversation with any Hungarian. It would seem to be their Mecca – its claim to fame being the biggest inland water in Europe. This is against all my cycling principles as it means putting a big south west 'zig' on my continuing easterly 'zag'. But the temptation has been irresistible. I am missing the Danube, so the lure of another big chunk of water is sufficient.

There is an unexpected diversion on the way when I spot two microlights in a field. The hot and boring bike ride is salvaged by a cool and spectacular fifteen minute flight which I can kid myself is free as it uses up the last of my German currency. It is also my fifty ninth birthday, so perhaps a treat is in order. Kitted up I find myself sitting at very close proximity behind the pilot, my legs all but wrapped around him. This is an unwelcome but unavoidable intimacy, which he capitalises on by pressing rather too often on my thighs as a means of checking if everything is OK. Certainly the noise from the engine, which all but serves as a headrest, makes conversation impossible but a thumbs-up would suffice. However, two thousand feet above ground is not a sensible time to bring up the issue of harassment.

Lake Balaton turns out to be nothing more than an oversized German lido and bitterly disappointing. Prices of everything from rooms to watermelons are inflated by a factor of at least three and are shockingly quoted in Deutsche marks without any mention of forint (Hungarian currency). Several enquiries at B&Bs establish this, and even had my budget permitted, there is no question of the proprietor allowing me to stay. The rooms are only let out to couples who would be staying for minimum of a week. I opt for one of the many campsites, each of which is the size of a small town. To complete my misery, a vicious gale blows up just about midnight and the tiny tent collapses, leaving me several hours of wide awake tension. I am worried that all that flapping might rip the material leaving me with a problem way beyond duct tape.

The tent had been blown over thanks entirely to the inadequate and now very bent pegs, so the time has come to replace them and I am confident that sturdy and long nails would be a perfect substitute. I track down a hardware shop in the next town and push my miming skills to the limit. Soon all the staff are gathered round watching my antics and after a few false starts where hammers and chisels are produced amidst incredulous looks, someone brings out a nail, but it is only an inch long. With more gesticulating and persuasion, and much to everyone's amazement, I triumphantly leave the shop having purchased eight nails each six inches long. They have seen my bike outside and cannot make a connection.

The day's ride is memorable. Cherry trees line the road and are dripping with juicy, sweet ripe fruit. This offers plenty of opportunity to stop and gorge; they are not just delicious, they are an excellent source of energy and rehydration. I also get the chance to slipstream a tractor. It overtakes me towing a large metal container and catching it means some exhausting sprinting but having done so, I can tuck in behind and cover the next fifteen miles effortlessly at a speed of eighteen miles an hour – the equivalent of supersonic. (To put this in perspective, my daily average speed is between ten and twelve miles per hour resulting from a great deal of pedal power.) Oh what satisfaction, and the bizarre truth is that the driver probably had no idea of my presence.

I am forced to book into an expensive hotel as the campsite shown on the map no longer exists, and the two old crones sitting in armchairs turn out not to be guests but employees and are not happy to have their gossiping interrupted. More sign language, assisted with drawings, maps and the calculator (the universal tool to establish the cost of the room and breakfast – and age) finally seals the deal. I don't think the place has had any guests since last year and I am made to feel a proper nuisance. The supper is disgusting but my need for calories means I have to eat it and there is no breakfast. This is my favourite meal of the day and I had been led to believe it is included in the non-negotiable price. I am ashamed to say that I seek revenge by stealing a pillow. This is very spontaneous theft and only possible because the pillow, soft and feathery, is about one third normal size. This is going to transform nights in the tent – a pillow has no substitutes. As I cycle away, it is not so much remorse that strikes me but a terror that my good luck could end. By now there is an undeniable feeling that I am being looked after and perhaps deliberate robbery would bring about retribution. Oh well, it's too late, the pillow is now part of The Team. Time will tell.

Red letter days are beginning to outnumber those which are less eventful, and my last full day in Hungary serves as an example. (It is always a challenge, indeed a necessity, to ensure that when leaving any country there are not pockets full of loose change or wads of cash left over.) I have the equivalent of £1 – not enough to pay for a campsite, never mind a room, so the plan is to pitch the tent in a field, eat the remains of my larder and get rid of the change by buying a coffee in the morning. That's the plan.

Mako is the last sizeable town before the Rumanian border and after a picnic on a bench in the crowded centre, I am wrongly directed out of town. It is my shadow that arouses suspicions. Depending on the time of day, it gives a very accurate clue as to which direction I am heading and it is indicating north east, whereas the road on the map is definitely east. This prompts me to stop at a factory gate several miles out of the town to check exactly where I am. The fearsome barking of the Alsatian guard dog unleashes an extraordinary chain of events which completely alters my plan.

Once Alex, the owner of the business, has recovered from the shock of not just my journey and my age but also the fact that I am intending to camp in a field, he takes over my life. Arrangements are made for me to stay in an old farmhouse just this side of the border which Geza, a friend of his is refurbishing, and he also invites me to join his family for supper this evening. The farmhouse is a perfect place to stay and Geza collects me later in the afternoon.

Before heading off for the meal, he takes me to meet his girlfriend who is on duty at Customs working a twelve hour shift checking the documentation of a never ending queue of huge articulated trucks. It is work she loathes but the money is good. We then stop off at two traditional bars – something of a treat for me not because of the alcohol but they represent a local way of life that I never otherwise get to see. Geza is keen for me to taste several brands of wine and sherry which I wisely keep down to thimble sized sips. What does grab my attention is the brisk take-away business being transacted. Customers arrive with three litre plastic Pepsi or Sprite bottles which are empty. They are filled with wine and then taken home.

The evening is warm and tranquil and we arrive to find the garden glowing in gentle light from dozens of candles and a superb barbecue with an accompanying feast of potatoes, vegetables, salads and bread. Alex and I discover that we share a recent birthday and the atmosphere takes off. Both daughters are studying English so for the first time in weeks most of the conversation is in English and my hands get a well earned rest. His friend then drives me back to the farmhouse where only his dogs are in permanent residence.

'Will you feel safe with just the dogs or would you like me to stay to protect you?' he asks. It would be catastrophic to allow any misinterpretation of 'protection', so I take my chances with the dogs. He returns in the morning before I'm packed and perhaps it's as well. By now a neighbour has discovered that I have slept in the house and is giving me the evil eye while I'm loading the bike. He puts the old man in the picture, whereupon his whole face lights up and they both stand waving goodbye with huge smiles.

Throughout Hungary deep concerns have echoed about travelling through Rumania and Bulgaria. It has become obvious that a definite pattern is forming. Each country perceives its neighbours as the baddies and dire warnings are unfailingly handed out about the dangers of travelling through the neighbouring country. Add to the equation a lone woman cyclist and the advice becomes emphasised and magnified. A perfect cameo of this conviction was portrayed by a young man serving in a Hungarian petrol station. I had specifically gone in to find a map of Rumania, which he pointed to on the rack. He had seen me arrive on a bike and with absolutely no verbal communication managed to convey his horror and concern that I should be asking for it. As an afterthought, I asked if there was also a map for Bulgaria. There was no misinterpreting the look of alarm on his face. I firmly believe that if he could have refused to sell it to me he would have done so!

With a happy heart and a surprisingly clear head, I set off for the border and the only problem which needs resolving is how to spend the £1. With temperatures consistently in the thirties and a couple of hours cycling under the wheels, a cold beer seems a far better option than a coffee. As you travel across Europe the size of coffee reduces in direct proportion to the cost increasing, whereas with beers it works in reverse. Smaller amounts of loose change buy larger glasses of chilled beer, far more appealing than a gritty thimbleful of luke warm coffee. As the first one has vanished with unladylike speed and used up less than half of the remaining change, a second is obligatory. I have been feeling distinctly apprehensive about this border crossing and the sight of the armed immigration officers offers no comfort. But the beers have done more than quench my thirst and get rid of my change. Having not eaten yet, I am experiencing a gentle euphoria and light-headedness (well, pissed, to be precise) – the perfect way of tackling such a moment of anxiety. The officials don't live up to their intimidating appearance of uniform and guns and I am treated with utmost civility. In a couple of minutes my dollar resources are minus thirty three – the cost of the visa – and that is that. For reasons which are inexplicable, the temperature leaps up several degrees in the space of a couple of miles and my usually tranquil and relaxing picnic is destroyed by a million revolting flies.

Chapter Five

The first night is determined from the map to be spent at a campsite south of Arad, a town which looks thoroughly uninviting from my saddle. But, once again there is no site – a scenario by now all too familiar and unbelievably infuriating. The only other option is an enormous hotel which is empty but for me. A certain repetitiveness about this, too. It is dilapidated and rundown, but there is evidence of past glory – palatial rooms and sumptuous furnishings – an opulence which is certainly not recent. The original furniture is in tattered ruins, the decor shabby and faded, fixtures and fittings are hanging off the walls and there are several floors of empty corridors and dusty surroundings. At least half the rooms must be out of commission, with signs of current work in progress out but no sign of any workmen.

Unlike the Hungarian crones, the two ladies working here are genuinely delighted to see me. Without a syllable in common, they understand something about my journey (maps are wonderfully useful on these occasions) and immediately halve their original quote for the room. It costs £2. They recognise that security of Alchemy is paramount and insist that the only place for the bicycle is in the room with me – a notable first. Then, surely beyond the call of duty, one insists on carrying the bicycle up to the second floor while the other gives me a hand with the heavy panniers. I feel incredibly safe and in spite of the rundown empty atmosphere the room is spotless. There is a wonderful touch of making-do where, in the absence of lace mats or table linen, there is a piece of kitchen roll under each bedside lamp. There are two single beds and I have to resist the impulse to lay Alchemy on one of them!

There is an urgency in the morning to get hold of local currency and food and the reception from people in the town at least matches the friendliness and generosity of spirit of any country so far. A couple of strangers lead me through the morning crowds to a money exchange. Without their help, finding this would have been impossible as the banks seem to have all been closed down, with heavy bars across windows and doors. Perhaps they ceased trading about the same time the hotel went into decline.

Until now I have been depending on that modern miracle – the hole in the wall that dispenses cash at the press of a button. Gone are the pressures of the need to set off abroad with wads of money and travellers cheques and all the accompanying anxieties. Instead, a small screen that communicates in at least three languages, dispenses cash in the local currency and finally states the balance in sterling. It is something that I never cease to marvel at. But, I had been aware before leaving that there would be countries where this facility would not exist and so have come prepared with a fistful, or more precisely a money belt full of dollars. Because of the incinerating temperatures the idea of 'belt' had to be discarded after the first week. The level of sweating had all but welded the notes together and the elastic bands securing them perished. The belt is now consigned to the depths of a pannier.

The deal is done and as 50,000 lei equals about £1.80 I could pretend huge wealth. Armed with Rumanian currency, I can now set about replenishing my larder.

Any commitment to health and hygiene has long since been abandoned, together with the belief that dairy products should be kept in a refrigerator or eaten immediately. It has seldom been below thirty degrees Centigrade since leaving, give or take several thunder storms, and I have adopted a system of buying provisions for at least a couple of days and strapping these on to the back rack with a couple of bungee chords. Without the luxury of cling film, plastic bags have to be recycled again and again and yet again. Bread rolls take on the consistency of bricks, bananas are mashed inside their skins, yoghurts become liquid and cheese metamorphosises into Play-Doh. A few days ago even my flexibility was stretched on unwrapping a mini Philadelphia cheese, nicked as surplus from breakfast, to find it a gentle shade of pink. But then I noticed it was labelled '*Fantasia*' and decided that pink was the intended colour, representing flavour rather than decay.

My idea of filling any one of the three water bottles with fruit juice could have proved very ill founded. Intended as a space saving device, the choice of which bottle was arbitrary and after a couple of weeks an ominous black mould was thriving inside all of them. In the absence of sterilizing kit and a bottle brush (just about the only tool missing on the Swiss army knife), some ingenious improvisation solved the problem. Each bottle was half filled with a cocktail of gravel and water and then rigorously shaken. Job done.

As one travels east, so the shops become harder to detect. Dressed window displays disappear along with all the accompanying clues as to what they sell. Instead, there are just small, often barred windows and any sign outside is meaningless. Compensating for the small ration of shops, there is an abundance of markets and roadside stalls and here the only danger is that of being ripped off. This first expedition in Vinga to buy food proves absurdly easy. German is still the common language (a state of affairs which is to remain true as far as Turkey) and as I am asking one pedestrian if he speaks English or German, a passer-by overhears me and interrupts. His German is fluent and soon I am following him through a maze of back streets. He has led me to a market where he instructs a friend to keep an eye on my bicycle while he negotiates prices with the various stall owners, keen to ensure that I am not overcharged. What he finds incomprehensible is that anyone could buy such small quantities. He obviously hasn't understood the concept of lack of space and refrigeration.

But more to the point, what an encouraging start. Absolutely everybody as far back as Germany has been warning how dangerous Rumania is.

It is the wind that proves hostile as I face the first testing, demanding slog. Strong, steady and head on, the climb up into the Carpathian Mountains is tough going and the surface of the road makes cycling even more difficult. The tarmac at the edges resembles a immobile choppy sea, significant and frequent undulations and in a heat resembling that of a furnace, it has melted. The consequent effect is pedalling along a mini roller coaster smothered in treacle.

In Timisoara I experience a minor accident and a monumental fright. The Team has pulled off the main road on to a slip road to check the map. I make the unforgivable error of pulling away from the curb without looking behind and head straight into the path of an older man also on a bicycle. Next thing I know is that Alchemy is flat on the road with me entangled in the frame and pedals. He has remained upright and unharmed but is rightly furious. Fortunately he accepts my signalled apologies which could not be more genuine or easy to interpret. He continues on his way, leaving me with a bloody knee, a jarred hip and trembling in shock for what might have been.... He could have been badly hurt and then the police would doubtless have been involved. I had made the mistake that so many pedestrians make when they step off pavements or leap from buses. Cars can be heard; bicycles cannot. A valuable and unnecessary lesson.

Local advice has recommended that a detour into one of the valleys is a must, so I head off to spend the night at Baile Herculane – a spa town with attitude. Since entering Rumania, evidence of extreme poverty has been the general order of things. Within the space of a few miles all this changes. Scarring the stunning landscape of magnificent mountains are huge skyscraper hotels, all doing a flourishing trade. There are certainly no £2 beds available here. Fortunately for my budget there is a campsite, although hardly recognisable in traditional terms with no caravans to be seen, never mind a tent. Instead, the couple of acres are covered with permanent cabins which are the homes of local men working in the resort. The man on duty is very happy for me to pitch my tent and confirms that this will be half the price of a cabin for the night, which is 80p. Even my need to be frugal can be waived here as I opt for the cleanliness, comfort and privacy of an idyllic log cabin.

There is plenty of time to enjoy the benefits of the spa, therapeutic and soothing to a body now showing signs of wear and tear, to say nothing of bloody blisters from that bloody saddle.

The evening is memorable as Rumania are playing Germany in Euro 2000 and the bar on site is revved up for the occasion, so I find myself sitting amongst about fifty male fans giving their team vociferous support. Surely those cries are the Rumanian equivalent of *are you blind, ref?* and *we were robbed* when they are refused an appeal for a penalty and the Germans win.

During the match I notice that a thirty something man is paying me more attention than the match. Sitting at the table in front of me, he turns every few minutes, looks and then quickly averts his eyes. There is no misinterpreting the interest and there is a bizarre inevitability that he would follow me when I return to my cabin later in the evening. What happens next is as endearing as it is comically pathetic, because he is not going to allow any lack of a shared language to get in the way of his efforts to chat me up. He proceeds on the basis that if he repeats the same words often enough, slowly enough and then again even more slowly, the message will finally be understood. The only romantic outcome of his best and very unthreatening endeavours is that I would certainly have missed the fireflies had he not pointed them out.

This could have been the opportunity to work on an idea put forward by a café owner. He had a theory that only alternative books sell and suggested that I should involve myself in an amorous liaison in each country to provide material on romantic male comparisons. A bit too alternative for my taste and the Brooks saddle would have made the venture a non-starter. So, instead, it is an easy choice to wish my suitor good night, light a stick of incense and meditate on my good fortune.

The hard work of yesterday is rewarded by an endless and gentle downhill ride amongst the mountains with ample time to take in the breathtaking scenery, culminating much to my delight alongside my old buddy, the Danube. Walnut trees line the deserted road for miles and miles providing welcome shade but sadly, unlike the cherries, the nuts are not ready to supplement my diet. I am reflecting on my good fortune, and mentally ticking off the stones which mark the distance in kilometres to the next town, as I approach a small village. Apart from the geese, there are four teenage youths a few hundred yards ahead and when they spot me they spread out across the road, join hands and begin to walk in my direction. One does not need to understand the language to realise that what they are shouting is abusive and any interpretation would be unwelcome. The tone is very threatening. Fortunately, there is no time to rationalise and think of alternatives – there are none. There isn't even time to remember all those warnings. Pure adrenaline accompanied by anger fire me up – how dare they. Shifting down to a lower gear I pedal like mad. Several hands try to grab hold of me, the panniers and the bike, but fail, and giving chase is never going to succeed. A bicycle, even with a middle aged woman on board, can out pace young lads over a longer distance. And so they are left behind, silent.

Luck was on my side as the road is flat. Had it been uphill the story could have ended differently. The question does spring to mind, just what would they have done had their spontaneous attack succeeded? I would have been rendered powerless and yelling for help would have proved fruitless as the local houses are screened by ten foot high solid walls. Their efforts to find anything worth stealing by rifling through the contents of the panniers would have made a spectacular mess of my luggage. The bike would without doubt have been a prize. What saved the day was my rage. Had I been overcome by fear, my legs would have turned to jelly making pedalling impossible. I would have fallen off without any help from them.

The words of one of my sons echoed loudly. While still at school, he and his friends were chased by a gang in Brighton. 'It is amazing just how fast you can run, Mum, when you have a bunch of Mods after you.'

And then, incredibly it happens in the next village and the one after that. Hallucinations in the heat – definitely not. Impossible to explain but nevertheless true. Each time the scenario is the same, as is the outcome.

Ironically it is barely an hour later that two policemen stop me to check my documents. They are lolling against a police car in the shade and are probably prompted to pull me over out of curiosity and boredom. It is from them that I learn that the only hotel this side of the border is closed for renovation.

Bang goes the master plan which was to stay on in Rumania for the night, ready to tackle Bulgaria early tomorrow morning. Several people I had talked to along the way suggested that it would make sense to hitch a lift through Bulgaria in one of the huge articulated trucks. The country undoubtedly has a comprehensive reputation of extreme danger extending beyond just its neighbours, so why not see it from the safety of an air conditioned cab and spend the saved time and money in Istanbul? The opportunity would present itself during the ferry ride to Vidin – the only way across. I have to confess that this has a certain appeal to it.

The mileage covered so far today is just short of one hundred and the prospect of having to continue even further is bad news. The good news is that there would be no lost sleep worrying about the challenge of an even more foreign border crossing. As it turns out, any thought of commandeering a lift is quite farcical. It is a short crossing and the small ferry carries barely twenty vehicles, most of which are tourists either in private cars or coaches. There are a couple of trucks but my courage fails completely. I justify my abject whimpishness with the fact that as they are both container trucks there would be nowhere to store a bicycle. Anyway, abandoning the idea is not a problem.

My anxieties about being intimidated at Customs once again turn out to be ill founded. The tourists are all made to disembark along with their luggage and are receiving some close scrutiny by armed men in uniform. For me it's different. A woman on duty inspects my passport and is curious about the loaded bicycle. As a result, she telephones several hotels in Vidin in an attempt to check the prices for rooms and book one for me. It is not at all encouraging to hear that there are no vacancies and camping is forbidden in Bulgaria. This is starting to feel scary and my insecurities are heightened on cycling into the town to realise that, because of Cyrillic script, it is impossible to understand fundamental signs such as 'hotel' or 'bank'. As so often, a pedestrian proves to be a perfect ally and leads me through several streets to a beautiful large and modern hotel where £10 buys a comfortable room and breakfast.

Top of priorities is what to do with Alchemy in this busy tourist hotel. The receptionist assures me that the parking area used for cars in the public square outside would be safe – a guard will be on duty throughout the night. I don't think so. She doesn't take much persuading that this is out of the question and agrees to allow the bicycle to go up in the lift to my fifth floor room. As the lift is miniscule, the task is something of a game show challenge because it means upending the poor bicycle (at least by now without panniers), much to the amusement of other guests. Fortunately, the hotel owner appears during this act of contortion and insists on unlocking a brand new shop in the reception area, due to begin trading next week, to house Alchemy for the night. The country that absolutely everybody had been warning me against travelling in has turned up trumps. I arrived barely an hour ago and already a customs officer has acted as a travel agent, a pedestrian as a city guide and the hotel owner and receptionist prove flexible and considerate. The kindness does not end there. The day is rounded off when Dutch tourists, travelling by coach through eastern Europe, encourage me to join them for the evening, treating me to beer, sandwiches and coffee.

A day of contrasts ends with mosquitoes putting in their first appearance. Had I known they would be my constant companions from now until half way across the southern States of America, I might well have turned around and gone back home. Their actual presence, rather than that of any perceived danger, is much more of a threat to my wellbeing. There is not an inch of my body that they don't manage to feast off during the coming months and waging war with chemicals proves a waste of time. The only effective protection is from coils which burn slowly for several hours. Leaving a window open for fresh air, even on the fifth floor (surely outer space in mosquito terms) guarantees their presence. They never fail to sense bare flesh. My greatest mistake comes in Turkey where, desperate to get sleep as they fight their airborne battle around my exhausted body, my tactic is to cover up entirely from nose to toes, leaving only my eyes and ears exposed. They hit their reduced target remorselessly and by morning both eyelids are swollen to the point of being almost closed and my ears resemble cauliflowers. The agony is second only to the humiliation – I resemble a defeated boxer and sunglasses offer no comfort.

With the temperature regularly registering over 40°C on my computer, drinking water has become even more of an issue. And what a relief not to have to buy it – at least not yet.

Everyone – shopkeepers, hairdressers, police or petrol stations, cafés, private homes – are only too happy to oblige, even bothering to put ice in. In spite of this thoughtful gesture, the water is usually luke warm and very unsatisfying to drink, bringing no feeling of respite from the heat and underlying thirst. The weird thing is that, although I am drinking enough each day to drown myself in, I never need to find a loo or a bush or a hedge. The liquid never reaches my bladder, gushing out instead through every pore in the form of gallons of sweat.

A scenario is played out during the morning that I would experience many times – the insuppressible male competitive urge. With roads in good shape, no traffic and open undulating countryside, I feel like the only person in the world until a cyclist overtakes me. At least my age, he is wearing a suit and holding a briefcase! He pedals past as if I am invisible but, as always happens on these occasions, it is not long before it is my turn to overtake him. The difference in our tactics is that my speed results from a regular rhythmic churning out of energy dictated by the topography combined with an excellent but heavy bicycle. By definition this results in The Team travelling more slowly up the hills but relatively fast going down. His speed is governed by his ego and once I am behind (out of sight) he has nothing to inspire and sustain him to greater efforts. So this leapfrogging fiasco continues for more than ten miles. The most bizarre part is that there is never any eye contact, never mind a smile. He puts in a final burst to ensure that he is ahead when he finally turns off.

And so it would continue in every country where bicycles are used. The signs are immediate – always this intense need to overtake without any acknowledgement, rather than the hundreds of others who would cycle alongside for a chat. It never bothers me. My insurance has a wonderfully superfluous clause which stipulates that there would be no cover if I were injured in a race (as if....) and because it usually happens over several miles, I find the predictability immensely rewarding and a welcome distraction.

The end of a particularly draining day sees me collapse in the shade of a café on the outskirts of Montana, desperate to buy an ice cold drink. Amongst the other customers are a group of three chaps and by one means or another I ask them if there are any cheap hotels in the town. Once again this casual contact prompts a remarkable reaction. They pull up a fourth chair and invite me to join them. During the next couple of hours they ensure an endless stream of drinks ranging from miniature cups of coffee to cokes and beer from the fridge, while we discuss via sign language and drawings not just which hotel would suit me best but precisely how to find it. ('Is that the sixth or seventh turning on the left?' all done with fingers and hand movements!)

They are horrified to learn that I intend to cycle over the Balkans to Sofia and go into lengthy consultation as to how this could most safely be achieved. These mountains are viewed as bandit country. They send me on my way armed not just with comprehensive hand drawn maps and phonetically written names, but also what must have been their supper. It is a bag containing fresh bread, several tomatoes, three hard boiled eggs, cheese and spring onions. They caution me to eat it all soon or throw everything away because of the heat, unaware of the liberties I have been taking so far. Their names and addresses are added to my note book. It is inspiring what sign language and frequent smiles can achieve.

About to hit the road in the early morning, the receptionist comes up with brilliant advice – let the train take the strain. She too is very concerned. It seems that even the Bulgarians view Bulgaria as dangerous. This might be construed as cheating, but to ignore the general consensus of the locals that the mountains conceal danger is beginning to seem foolhardy. And the great benefit would be avoiding several days of mountainous roads and the real prospect of not reaching a hotel before dark, so without much agonising the choice is made.

My stay at the hotel has been highlighted thanks to the presence of a young lad employed there. When I arrived he was at the entrance to take all my panniers to the room and ensure the bicycle was safely locked up for the night.

During our long chat yesterday evening his colloquial English prompted the question 'How did you learn to speak such excellent English?' The level of conversation had far exceeded *'how old are you'* as he enthused over my journey.

And the answer – 'I learn everything from Michael Jackson records'.

His hobby is his mountain bike and he was very keen to know how much Alchemy cost. Realising that the truth might be shocking, it was evident that a lie was needed and so naively I decided to knock off about one third replying '£1,000'. On seeing his stupor, I lied again saying the cost was in dollars. At the time I felt an element of shame, wondering just how many months' wages this would represent to him but to his credit he refrained from finding the words from his Michael Jackson vocabulary to castigate me.

(This was the first of many occasions that this question would arise, always asked by young men. Wiser and keen not to offend, the amount drops dramatically to $250 but this still generates reactions of disbelief, so as a last resort I complete the lie by saying it had been a present from my family and I hadn't got a clue.)

He has brought his bike in this morning to show me – his pride and joy – along with a large glass jar of fresh yoghurt and second containing home made strawberry jam from his family farm. The receptionist holds Alchemy while he clips on the panniers and offers to guide me out of town. Before leaving, the serious challenge is securing the yoghurt and jam safely in my larder. Carrying anything made of glass on a bike is not recommended, but to leave these items behind would have been deeply hurtful. The bungee chords were a small investment but there is no end to their versatility. He accompanies me well beyond the outskirts of the town and is very reluctant to turn back. He would surely come to Istanbul if it were possible.

The station is in the next town, some twenty miles away and the train does indeed take the strain. The only time I break sweat is loading the heavy bicycle from a barely existent low platform up four deep and steep steps into the carriage but there are plenty of willing hands to help. With no guards van to secure the bike, it is necessary to stand in the corridor and so I perch on the crossbar and am not surprised to find it more comfortable than the saddle. The mountains pass painlessly in a couple of hours at a cost £1.20.

Since leaving home I have travelled without the relevant Rough Guide or Lonely Planet, specific to each country and a backpacker's bible, relying instead on synchronicity and instinct, neither of which takes up precious space or adds unwelcome weight. It has worked remarkably well to date. The challenge of finding a cheap hotel in the capital Sofia without such an encyclopaedia might have proved impossible but once again a stranger steps in. On this occasion it is a taxi driver waiting in a taxi rank who spots me peering through the filthy windows of a derelict tourist information office and comes over to ask what it is I want. He then locks his taxi and leads me around a couple of corners to introduce me to a nearby hotel, something I would never have achieved by myself. Unlike the huge, modern and expensive global counterparts, these places are behind locked and barred doors looking nothing like a hotel to a passing Western tourist. He helps carry The Team up the stairs, checks that there is a suitable room, negotiates a discount and then returns to his rank, expecting nothing. Once I'm washed and sorted, the hotel owner seeks me out to escort me to the ATM so that I can withdraw cash without being intimidated and then vacates his office to allow me to use his computer to send an email back home.

Buoyant on the success of the train, it seems eminently sensible to leave Sofia in the same fashion – a strategic as well as cowardly choice. The purpose is to avoid the hell of navigating my way out of a sprawling city and negotiating the appalling road surfaces made up of craters with Galactic black hole proportions which are very capable of damaging Alchemy's wheels. This also means escaping the trauma of the continuous twenty four hour traffic chaos where a cyclist becomes part of real life game of dodgems.

The receptionist has checked the train time and armed me with various pieces of paper with such questions as *'please may I have a ticket to Plovdiv for me and my bicycle'* and *'please could you tell me which platform the train from Plovdiv leaves from?'* This is written in Cyrillic on one side and in English on the other, such was her concern and meticulous attention to detail. Lulled into a sense of false security, I arrive at the station with plenty of time to spare and confidently head for the ticket sales window.

An hour's complete nightmare follows whereby the neatly written request for a ticket brings nothing but abusive shrugs, grunts, folded arms, pointing fingers and even a back turned. Has the French Tourist Board been giving lessons? I become utterly confused. Why no ticket? It is early and the commuter rush hour is in full flood, so undaunted I stand amongst the hurrying crowds and shout 'Does anyone speak English or German?' And miraculously nobody does (this is a first), or maybe they just don't want to admit to it. They are after all trying to catch a train to get to work and the average commuter, however altruistic, does not leave time to spare.

Out of the crowd, two men smartly dressed in suits come to my aid, which is tricky as we share not a single word of common language. My scraps of paper put them in the picture and the three of us plus Alchemy re-enact the whole cycle. At least negotiating the four flights of tortuous stairs is easier with two extra pairs of strong hands. After much discussion with the uniformed Job's Worth behind the glass, we head off to the parcels office downstairs and it gradually dawns on me what all the commotion is about. My bicycle and the panniers qualify as *'a parcel'* and not only would they have to travel separately, but on a different train.

Risking my life amongst potholes and traffic is as nothing compared to the risk of never seeing Alchemy and my luggage again. Without a nano second's hesitation, the train idea becomes history. The only way I can convey my rejection of the plan is to shake my head and spread my hands in a gesture of helplessness. The two men are utterly shocked and bemused. They have spent the last half an hour sorting the confusion and obviously have faith in the honesty and efficiency of the railway system. It is impossible to explain to them that in no circumstances could the separation of me from the bicycle and panniers be an option.

'Ungrateful bitch' surely reflects their thoughts as The Team slowly walk away. I just hope they haven't missed their train.

The twenty two miles of hellish navigating and cycling to clear Sofia proves if nothing else that the idea of the train had been a good one and I eventually end up illegally on a motorway expecting to hear police sirens at any minute. My supersonic heartbeat reflects my panic and not the effort of pedalling. The misery of the day is completed at the hotel in Pazardzik. Due to the mix and match of sign language and German, my initial understanding was 35 levit for a room, no breakfast. My room in the capital city of Sofia was only 30 levit. Then I realise that the receptionist is talking in dollars. This is extortion by any standards but the best I can do is ask for the manager and negotiate down to $28. With no other choices and camping forbidden, that spot between a rock and a hard place offers a better alternative and at least would be free. Bulgaria's accommodation is proving more expensive than France.

It is game, set and match to the hotel when, having paid in dollars, the change is given to me in levit. As sarcasm doesn't translate into sign language, it is impossible to register my disgust at this absurd inconsistency. Amongst the room's furnishings are a broken television and a Fifty's record player. Just how many hotel guests, even if they arrive by car, would be carrying their favourite selection of long playing records? But it's odds on that it too doesn't work. Determined that the hotel will not benefit to the tune of a single further levit, I buy a delicious supper of fresh fruit from the local market. It comes as no surprise in the morning when the surly night porter continues to watch football on his television and ignores my struggles to get through swing doors and down the steps. What a difference a day makes.

Defining the ladies and gents loos is proving intriguing. Perhaps with the knowledge that nobody in the whole world speaks their native language, Hungarians, Rumanians and Bulgarians have opted for symbols on each door to ensure that mistakes are not made. Apart from the more obvious outline of a male and a female, Hungary uses a silhouette of a man standing at a urinal and a woman sitting on a pedestal, whereas Rumania chooses a more tasteful and subtle outline of the appropriate shoe! Without going into too much detail, discovering where the flush is situated could take longer than the deed itself. I have to wait until America to experience the extraordinary and somewhat unnerving self-flushing loos.

Tea in Bulgaria is so cheap that it cannot even be considered an expense. I use it as an ideal excuse to stop for a rest and drink it whenever possible. Always fruit rather than black tea, it is served piping hot. As I am adding either sugar or salt to everything I consume these days, it is a refreshing sweet drink. The coffee is disgusting comprising two mouthfuls of grit and grinds.

My salivating anticipation for breakfast each day is beyond any food experience ever. If it is not part of the cost of a room, I make an early start in a futile attempt to avoid the heat and with a couple of hours cycling behind me, this first meal always centres around cheese omelette, chips, hot bread and salad. Cafés of every description serve up wonderfully fresh and good value food where someone unfailingly joins me with the familiar question – *'how old are you?'* – and the familiar warning – *'the next country is dangerous'*.

On this occasion I stop at a transport café and it is a Turkish truck driver who pesters me. At first it seems that his thick German accent is influenced by his native language, until it dawns that he is just very drunk. And about to drive a huge articulated truck to Greece. (Some days ago truckers in another café tried lifting my bicycle with the four panniers attached off the ground. When they returned to the table one of them felt my calves as they made jokes about my strength. It was very unchauvanistic and light-hearted and everyone joined in the laughter. That was as far as the touching went.)

Map reading has become my obsession and many hours are spent studying routes. Distance is the crucial factor. My daily average has settled at sixty seven miles, but this could reduce dramatically given a mountain or two or much worse, a persistent head wind. Alternatively, flattish and no wind or a heaven sent tail wind, then well over eighty is possible. The whole exercise is centred around the next night stop.

What has caught my attention on this final leg to the Turkish border is about fifteen miles designated *'motorway'* status. The main roads in Hungary had signs forbidding cyclists but the police chose to turn a blind eye and I had already pushed my luck leaving Sofia by cycling right under the noses of a police watchtower without being spotted. It is imperative not to live through that heart-racing fear again. Producing my map, I ask the truck driver for help but we never get passed the question of my age and married status.

Anticipating problems, images have been flooding my head. Scenarios range from being arrested and never seen again, having Alchemy confiscated, being redirected to another border hundreds of miles away, or at best just fined (in dollars no doubt). Typical of all my worries, nothing could be further from the truth. The map has lied – it is not a motorway, just a trunk road and amongst those travelling on it are chickens, geese, sheep, cows and peasant farmers walking alongside carts being pulled by donkeys. Motorised occupation is made up of dozens of mopeds, an occasional tractor and rarest of all a car. The paradox is that not a single TIR truck looms over the horizon so the source of any pollution is that of methane rather than exhaust fumes.

Chapter Six

Another border, this time with a hectic pedestrian trade far in excess of any vehicles. They are all men who cross into Turkey on a daily basis to go to work and maintaining my place in the queue becomes a battle. Adopting a filthy glare and using The Team as a battering ram (so much more effective than elbows) I bump and barge, snarling 'don't even think about it' at any pushy man. On entering Bulgaria I was given a carnet which had to be stamped by each hotel I stayed at and so this is collected. Business is completed with the purchase of a £10 Turkish tourist visa. By now I have come to the conclusion that the cost of any visa is arbitrary. It seems a very effective way of demanding money without argument – bureaucratic mugging.

I am about to discover the value of a travel book as *'Asia Overland'* will soon become my bible. Turkish Immigration have been known to turn a traveller away if they don't have the exact money for this visa. Not even two £5 notes will do if the man behind the desk is having a bad attitude day. My passport is presented at least ten times while negotiating a mile of gates and lanes, not a car or truck in sight. Feeling incredibly excited, it seems appropriate to take a photograph of the customs officers who are keen to ask me questions and want to hold Alchemy. Their refusal is adamant and nothing to do with being camera shy. It is such a disappointment as it is a huge moment.

(On my return to England I would reflect on many such occasions. My camera is used frequently but the photographs never reflect the instants of extreme emotions or achievements. For example, it was impossible, of course, to capture any of the three occasions when four boys had tried to knock me off nor would it be possible to photograph the chasing Mexican dog intent of having my heels for supper. Photographs of views, campsites, people met along the way have limited interest to anyone but me.)

Before tackling the ATM in a country for the first time it is vital to have a handle on the rate of exchange. Guessing can do serious damage to your bank account. It is not as if the money can be shoved back down the hole in the wall if you have estimated incorrectly. Transformation to millionaire status is assured in Turkey, but thanks to a nought too far and sun blindness, mine is greater than intended. The sun is beaming full blast directly on to the screen obliterating all information. Even the locals are struggling as no amount of close peering and hand cupping does any good. My intention is to draw out the equivalent of £20 but the addition of an extra nought spills forth so much paper I am grateful there was no howling gale. Squishing the well used notes into my money belt stretches it to capacity.

Having been thwarted with the train ride out of Sofia, an unshakeable decision has been made to catch a bus to Istanbul. The two hundred and twenty kilometres through uninspiring landscape along busy roads represents three days' cycling. But first the bus station has to be found. Situated always on the outskirts of a town, I am convinced I have overshot so I pull in to where three men are sitting in an empty warehouse reading the paper and playing backgammon. No English from them and no Turkish from me, so out comes the book to show them the highlighted word for bus station – 'otogar' – some preparation paying off here. Before even attempting to answer, however, they sit me down, offering choices of 'chai', coffee or cold mineral water. Continuing our conversation in sign language, they reveal that England had beaten Germany in Euro 2000. The day is definitely turning out well. Suitably calmed down and revived, I have to retrace my wheel tracks as I have indeed missed the bus station and with still no sign, I ask again. This time it is three men eating outside a café and they invite me to share their lunch. Tempting as it is, there is a strong sense of urgency to board this bus, if it can be found.

And the rest is so blissfully easy. For the equivalent of £5, The Team is safely and simply packed away in one of the spacious holds underneath, my bum feels the joy of a comfortable seat, hot tea and cold drinks are on regular offer from a stewardess and the kilometres pass in air conditioned luxury in two and half hours.

But what goes around comes around. The otogar in Istanbul is also on the outskirts of the vast city so the journey into the centre is not a matter of a couple of miles along a main road. It is twelve miles – if you know the way. Navigating through an unchartered maze of urban sprawl occupied by manic traffic prompts an adrenaline rush never achieved on any funfair ride. Hardly able to find the exit of the bus station, how would I succeed finding Istanbul's old town? With the ever strengthening feeling that Alchemy's are the first bicycle tyres to have touched this tarmac, my appeals for directions amongst the hundreds of people inhabiting the bus station go unheeded. I am clearly a thorough nuisance and am left to negotiate the various levels and exits on a trial and error basis.

With my shadow as my trusty guide, I set off south east amidst rush hour traffic speeding from every angle, the air filled with exhaust fumes and the sound of hooting, which I initially mistake as being directed at my unwelcome presence. Driving culture has resulted in the horn replacing the use of the brakes, which are surely fitted as an optional extra. The 'Topkapi' sign brings a degree of comfort as it proves I am on course and I am just daring to relax, only to find the road swooping into a long tunnel – very spooky – the other end of which develops into a four lane (each way) carriageway. My vulnerable team is in the middle of a terrifying tarmac jungle with no escape. In the meantime my shadow has revolved through one hundred and eighty degrees which means I am headed back to where I've just come from.

What happens in the next fifteen minutes would not be for those of a nervous disposition. Suffice to say that to stand any chance of getting back on track it is necessary to scurry amongst the traffic with an unwieldy bicycle, still unsure which way to go as the four lanes then split into two plus two, mirrored by the carriageway going in the opposite direction. Ricocheting from one lane to another, dodging between oncoming cars (now the angry hooting is definitely directed at me), hauling the bike over several concrete barriers, pushing exhausted up a slip road with cars rushing towards me (all of this without a pavement in sight), staying alive becomes more important than finding the right road. The reward is the magnificent sight of a long straight boulevard with a tram line, shops and people. I recognise its name and description from the travel book and know I am miraculously back on course.

Eventually, thrill of thrills I arrive in Sultanahmet, the old city, and it is only mid-afternoon so all that remains is to find somewhere to stay. With the prospect of applying for the visa to Iran, I know this will probably have to be at least a couple of weeks, so it is important to get it right and my book has given me some ideas. To escape a hotel tout in this neighbourhood would mean being deaf, blind and dumb or the use of frequent slapping and foul language. They saturate the pavements, their sole purpose being to lure tourists to the hotel which pays them commission in the form of free accommodation and food and explains their tenacity and rhino-like skin. In spite of my determination to remain independent, any attempt to pursue my search unaided is no match to their pestering and capitulation is inevitable. Thus, having meekly followed one of them, by five o'clock the Paris Hostel has benefited from millions of my Turkish lire, discounted on the promise that the stay will be for at least three nights. Apple chai, chai, coffee and Internet access are available free of charge. All that is needed to benefit from any of these perks will be electricity, which is to prove something of a luxury during the coming days.

On arrival the staff are very friendly and carry Alchemy and the panniers to my room on the third floor. If they speak English at all it is of the kebab variety – heavily influenced by Turkish.

One in particular is very attentive and he is the first Turkish person whose name I ask 'Ali Baba' is his reply. Is this a childhood dream?

I am in the overcrowded sitting room choking on cigarette smoke with the television blaring out a football commentary when he suggests the roof would be more pleasant. Dragging me up six steep flights of stairs and carrying a freshly made apple chai specially for me, all becomes clear. The most glorious panorama of the Bosphorus with vivid blue sea and dozens of boats ranging from ferries to cruise ships – a picture postcard view. I am about to settle down when for the third time today three men have other ideas. My refusal is ignored as they are adamant that I join their picnic of water melon, feta cheese, fresh bread, very salty (even for my taste) peanuts and Raki. My diary can wait as the evening passes in perfect surroundings, although I have great difficulty in persuading them that I am not remotely tempted by the Raki. Euro 2000 is still attracting a large audience and on returning downstairs some time later, I join the men to watch England being beaten by Rumania. The residents cannot contain their glee when Rumania are awarded a penalty – England is not popular because of the antics of the hooligan fans. When it's all over the hotel night staff cook a veggie pasta and again I find myself a guest at the table of strangers.

During the coming weeks the presence of an American, Mark, turns out to be the real bonus. A seasoned traveller, he favoured this hotel because it does not feature in any of the travel books which means that backpackers rarely stay (unless captured by the tout) and it has more of a local flavour. He is at the start of a four month trip around Turkey and is a font of knowledge and wisdom. We share the common interest of preferring to avoid accepted tourist pastimes, most especially sightseeing. It is so comforting when he tells me that people back home in the States become really angry on discovering that he hasn't visited local historical sites. There is an implied accusation that he has failed or done something very wrong. Immediately I feel better and tell him about Csaba.

His succinct observation on learning about the agony inflicted by the Brooks saddle is 'Well, you've just got to look at it to know it's going to be uncomfortable'.

I am beginning to get a whiff of the Emperor's new clothes.

Chapter Seven

If the idea of tackling those borders in Eastern Europe had felt daunting, it is nothing compared to what is about to follow. So far visas have been obtained on arrival, although the charge varied greatly. The countries in Asia through which my intended journey is routed all need a visa prior to arrival, which means visiting the relevant embassy in the adjacent country. Iran and Pakistan are at the top of the list. Without these, a radical re-think is on the cards.

At a guess, probably at least thirty of the forty beds in the hostel are occupied by Iranians working in the city and the manager, Nasim, has assured me that he has a special relationship with the consul at the Iranian Embassy.

'No problem, Pam.'

Such a contact seems an astonishing stroke of luck; or more of that synchronicity. The drama unfolds in fits and starts over the next three weeks. My initial escort comes in the form of inmates of the 'Paris', three of the most scruffy, scrawny and downtrodden men. On arrival we find the Embassy closed which is particularly puzzling as according to Nasim, the consul himself is expecting me; an appointment has been made. But, as nobody apart from myself speaks a word of English and there are rather too many scowling faces and guns for my liking, it is pointless trying to explain to the security guards at the gate, never mind argue.

My mission has become common knowledge amongst the residents of the hostel, one of whom volunteers to accompany me. Varol is an extraordinary cocktail: a Turk who has been brought up in Denmark and earned his living for many years in England. If it is possible for the dice to be loaded in such a venture, mine certainly appear that way. With Nasim able to smooth the bureaucratic formalities and Varol to act as interpreter, it surely will be *'no problem'*. My contribution is a photo of myself in a veil.

Opening times are random and bear no relation to information posted at the main entrance, so it takes four attempts just to get inside. And then – simply entering the room is enough to destroy any confidence, which vanishes before the door shuts. Looking as if they've been there for days, several comatose men are slumped on benches, but Varol and I choose to remain standing. More people continue to arrive. Half an hour elapses before life in the shape of a solitary clerk appears behind the glass. Instantly everyone crushes up against the counter – queuing and discipline do not belong here. It is all about brute force and barging and makes the queue at the border look like a kindergarten playground. A woman would stand no chance, never mind one who speaks neither Turkish nor Iranian. Tempers and frustration are exacerbated with the disappearance of the clerk at frequent and lengthy intervals. Without Varol I might well have fled, striking Iran off my agenda. Whatever travelling through the country might entail, it could never be as scary as the angry crowd in this cramped room. The next couple of hours involve good use of our elbows, yelling, barging, grabbing the attention of the man behind what looked like bullet proof mirrored glass, filling in terrifying forms and parting with $50. Stressful would not do justice to this encounter but promises from everyone concerned (including the main man who has spoken to Varol on the phone) are that ten to fourteen days would see it through, instead of the normal twenty five. My confidence soars – it is always about who you know. There is an ominous observation about the $50 being unrefundable.

To obtain the Pakistan visa I need a *'letter of recommendation'* from the British Embassy which brings about the only daylight robbery of my journey, not as might be imagined being mugged on my way there. No, instead the legitimate extortion of £35 to produce such a letter in my name – a simple mail merge on a word processor to recommend someone who has just walked in off the street carrying a British passport. Outrageous, but not negotiable.

As Mark put it 'You expect to get screwed when travelling – but not by your own government.'

While waiting for my letter, the Scottish chap working there discovers the background to my request and promptly launches into a familiar speech about the dangers involved.

'You should not even consider cycling alone in Turkey' is his unequivocal advice.

He then elaborates with the old themes of woman on her own, blah blah blah and backs this up with a three hundred page document titled *'Advice to Travellers in Turkey'* which he wants me to stop and read. Does he expect me to abandon my journey on the strength of this advice? Go home because he says so? I do understand that it is said in good faith and with good intentions, but....

'To be honest' I reply 'what you are saying is nothing new. It has a very familiar ring to it as I have been hearing similar words about every country more or less since I left home. But I've chosen to ignore the advice. If I hadn't I would have been back in England long ago, in fact probably never left. I appreciate that you feel it's your duty to pass on such perceived wisdom, and it's not that I don't appreciate it. But it's so far, so good and I do believe that someone up there is on my side. It does helps that I don't have the imagination to frighten myself, but thanks anyway.'

He shrugs his shoulders and says 'I think you're very unwise. Don't say I didn't warn you.'

'Oh, don't take any notice of him.' One of his colleagues has overheard our conversation and adds 'He always like to see the worst side of things. I'm sure you'll be absolutely fine.'

Someone sensible at last, or at least living up to the maxim of live and let live.

Armed with my expensive document, the mission almost fails as it takes most of the morning to track the Pakistan Embassy down. Both the other two were substantial buildings.

The British was pristine with landscaped gardens, the Iranian dilapidated with the walls covered in everything including what looked like bullet holes. Both had heavily armed security guards and a very high fence. Finding this last one proves so difficult that there is a strong possibility that a visit to the country might have to be forfeited. No embassy, no visa, no visit. Would I get a refund on my £35 letter? Assuming wrongly that it would fall in to the *'impossible to miss'* category and navigating from an out of date (but not realised at the time) tourist information map, it is a close call. Taxi drivers, police, shopkeepers, pedestrians – nobody can help.

The reason finally becomes clear – it occupies a couple of rooms on the third floor of an office block. No guards, but straight into a room with one man behind a counter. It looks more like a bookies. My good fortune is that there are no other customers, Pakistan visas clearly not in great demand. A bit of a clue here, I feel. The dreaded forms are filled out in triplicate without the aid of carbon paper. Form blindness is something that everyone more or less suffers from but these are serious documents and cannot be skipped through. He scans it, relieves me of $55 and his attitude transforms the instant he hears about my journey. Far from exhorting me to take up knitting or something more suitable to my gender and age, he enthusiastically recommends places to go in Iran, having served as consul there for several years, as well as what to do or not do to stay safe in Pakistan. He advises strongly to take buses to get past some of the more remote and dangerous areas. He even goes so far as to spend several minutes sketching maps and writing out names. I can't wait. By the time I leave we are best buddies.

Having to pace myself in Istanbul is made more enjoyable in the company of Mark and Varol. It means that meals become a social part of each day. Eating with others is always so much more satisfying and enjoyable than eating on one's own. I am very aware of having lost a great deal of weight since leaving England and with my appetite and stomach now in unison eating is a real pleasure. It is indeed a revelation to realise how much restraint normally rules my choices. Now there is nothing that I could not eat without a twinge of guilt or the dreaded thought '*I shouldn't really*'.

The sight of Turkish men holding hands does take some getting used to; a practice which extends as far as policemen on duty. It is not unusual to see a man with his hand on the knee of another, or even massaging the back of his neck while watching the football on television. All this has no sexual connotations; it is just the culture. I am developing a strong suspicion that everyone in the country smokes and owns a mobile.

An indication of the technological revolution taking place was demonstrated on checking *Asia Overland* for information about ATMs and Internet cafés. It was only published two years previously and indicates that there is just one of each of these facilities in Istanbul. Not so in July 2000. Both the holes in the wall and the email facilities are to be found not just on every street corner, but in the most of the buildings in between. It wouldn't have been surprising to find a few tucked away amongst the ancient ruins. The Turks do not miss a trick when it comes to taking money off you.

'*Visa day*' arrives and the hanging around proves all to no avail. Promises, promises and Turkish bullshit – no Turkish delight this time. The regular doses of '*no problem*' from the hostel manager turn out to be one of the only two English phrases he knows. That would be perfectly acceptable if the sentiment were backed up with knowledge – a bit of insider dealing would go down a treat. But his 'no problem', spoken in whatever language, proves meaningless. A parrot in a cage could have had more sincerity and wouldn't have shrugged its feathers and laughed on hearing that the visa has been denied, and then ask on drawing the next breath 'How are you Pam?' – his other phrase. As my immediate plans have dissolved, two unnecessary weeks have been spent hanging around, almost more money has disappeared in this time than in the whole of the journey so far – how the hell does he think I am? The promise evaporated, along with my non refundable $50 and the only consolation is that all those family and friends who have been so concerned about this stage could now relax.

It does need to be strongly emphasised, however, that I later encounter many others who have travelled through Iran and received extraordinary hospitality and kindness. Their experiences in the country rated amongst their most memorable highlights. So, after the big Iranian thumbs down, my instinct is to catch the first flight to Pakistan. Turkey, or more specifically, several of its inhabitants have caused me a massive sense of humour failure.

This is delayed thanks to a fortuitous intervention by Simon. He arrived on the roof of the hostel with the most appalling dyed red hair, the result of a lost bet, having been recommended to come and talk to me as he is looking for advice on cycling back to the UK! He is also keen to check out the Black Sea area and so we both willingly abandon our single status, in terms of travelling and cycling, and head off in that direction. The Black Sea has several attractions. It would hopefully be cooler than anywhere south, it is not a tourist area, being more the place that the Turkish people visit for their holidays and by all accounts the scenery is spectacular.

The ride compensates to some extent for the disappointment in not having to cross the whole country. The scenery is all that it is cracked up to be with magnificent forested mountains plummeting down to the clear and anything but black sea – stunning to view but tough to cycle.

The evenings are littered with kindness from locals as they watch our unlikely duo pedal into the village or town seeking to pitch our tents on the beach. En route to the coast a young group of lads rescue us one evening from a pestering hotel tout intent on taking $20 off each of us. They offer instead a free room in a partially built apartment block belonging to one of their fathers. They feed us on freshly cooked pitta stuffed with mince, onions and potatoes and invite us to join the audience listening to their band.

Another time a couple of young men drive us into town to buy supper, staying with us to ensure that the restaurant charges us local prices, rather than the *'whatever you can get away with'* price. A Muslim family picnicking on a beach insist we join them in the late afternoon and we are treated to the extraordinary spectacle of the fully shrouded women paddling, their bare ankles the only flesh visible. An engagement party which has taken over a beach café invite us to celebrate with them. A young couple who run a pharmacy drive us to their shop for coffee late one evening. This is done spontaneously, as are all these generous offers, but the occasion is spoiled by my concerns that we have left all our possessions in the tents. What if.... Tents are impossible to secure and we have been very high profile since our arrival as Simon spent a couple of hours offering rides on his bike to an ever increasing group of young teenage boys.

One evening things take a very nasty turn. Again, set up to sleep in our tents amidst many curious onlookers, two of the local police force arrive on the scene. Their heavily armed presence indicates that they are not looking for a test ride on a bicycle, nor is there an invitation to pitta and coffee back at the station. Their interest lies solely in Simon's passport, which he chose to leave in the hotel safe in Istanbul for security reasons. The police speak not a single word of English so at least we are spared the by now tedious and irritating innuendos about our relationship, but it also makes even a simple explanation of the absent passport impossible. The effectiveness of sign language has distinct limitations. These uniformed intruders become very threatening and after a great deal of pushing and shoving, they escort Simon to their jeep and drive off, leaving me shaking and bewildered. What next?

The drama is over in a couple of hours – plenty of time for mind games with no guaranteed happy ending. At one point the Job's Worth policeman returned with his colleague and asked to see my passport which he then grabbed and gestured that he was going to take it away in his jeep. With no intention of allowing this to happen, my instinctive reaction was to snatch it back, so a fierce tug of war ensued and when the passport ended up in my trembling hand, he threatened me by pointing repeatedly and rapidly at both his gun and his badge snarling 'Police'. My reply is unprintable.

A wonderful dimension to my daily ride has been the unexpected wild life, a welcome bonus which a cyclist has plenty of opportunity to appreciate and enjoy. The most unexpected and definitely the largest birds were the storks throughout Germany. It was nesting time and while sitting with a group of German cyclists, who had treated me to the most delicious coffee and cream cake, we watched the juvenile birds tentatively taking off, gliding in a huge circle and then landing again on their precarious home. I sighted many others perilously placed on the top of church towers, telegraph poles or even trees. Hares, with hind legs that would have done a kangaroo credit, had scampered along the cycle path ahead of me. In Laos I would see snakes sunning themselves on the road. Later, in Mexico, I was to spend an entire afternoon surrounded by butterflies. Less popular had been a morning in France when I was pebble dashed by a million black flies. The size of full stops, my shirt and shorts were covered with their corpses while others drowned in the sweat on my bare arms and legs. A flock of sheep caused a moment of satisfaction and humour in Hungary. They had escaped on to a busy main road and the traffic was backed up in both directions for several miles with hot and frustrated motorists hooting, yelling and getting out of their cars . Police were on the scene but proving completely ineffective and the farmer, relaxed and unembarrassed, wandered casually behind with his dogs. Nothing could persuade the sheep to hurry. Being on a bike I was unimpeded and could chuckle as I pedalled past.

But in Turkey this the wild life trail takes on a gruesome dimension – the dead life trail. This unwelcome trend continues throughout every country from now on, including the States. It is just the animals that vary, the vast majority being dogs and occasionally cats but the list includes birds, frogs, snakes, armadillos and raccoons. The largest and most shocking is a donkey lying right in the centre of the road and clearly not asleep. I was also horrified to witness a dog being hit by a car. The animal was left screaming in the road as the driver disappeared without a backward glance. With such an assortment and abundance of dead animals littering the road, it is not only important to avoid them but vital to take a very deep breath as you pass by – the decaying smell is utterly disgusting and repulsive. It could sometimes be a deeply disturbing experience.

Amazingly, cows escape the carnage. Throughout India they wander aimlessly along intensely busy roads but, considered sacred by Hindus, they are safe. To be born a cow in India means a guarantee to die of old age, although when I come to see how pathetically thin they are as they search for food on traffic islands in Delhi, breathing air black with pollution, an abattoir seems a preferable alternative. There are rumours that the cows are forced to roam the streets because they are expensive to feed once they cease to be productive. Their sacred status certainly brings them no quality of life.

Perhaps they could take lessons from a cow in Turkey who has adapted to modern life by perfecting an amazing trick. Simon and I have stopped for a wonderful breakfast of fresh bread, cheese and tomatoes at a large picnic site adjacent to a football field. The litter bins are overflowing and we watch this cow deliberately tip a bin over so that all the tied plastic bags inside spill out. Then, going down on its front knees with its bum in the air, it proceeds to rip a bag open, give it a vigorous shake and eat the remnants of someone else's picnic. Evolution on the hoof.

In Sinop I bump into a German who joins the list of those vehemently advising me to avoid Pakistan.

'I've been travelling around the world since the Sixties and have been to most countries in Africa and South America, as well as all over Asia, but Pakistan – never ever would I go there. It is asking for trouble, full of fanatics and religious fundamentalists. No traveller can expect to be safe and as a woman you are mad to even consider it. You would be lucky to get away with just armed robbery. It could be much worse – rape, kidnap, who knows. You really shouldn't go to Pakistan. No, nothing would ever persuade me to visit that country. Trust me, I know what I'm talking about.'

Coming from a seasoned rather than armchair traveller, his words hit more of a chord. My plans do not change (after all there is £75 invested in this visa) but I do wonder. It is comforting to meet an equally well seasoned Canadian traveller who has nothing but good to say of the place and is jealous that he cannot join me.

Chapter Eight

Packing up my tent for the last time in Turkey prompts memories of just how well it has served me. Camping has never been a part of my life and here in my sixtieth year I have slept under canvas for at least two thirds of my journey through Europe. I love the independence it gives me and the significant saving of money is welcome. At the end of each day the biggest hazard is tiredness and often with my sarong spread on the ground, I would collapse in the shade and relax for an hour. Such is the technology of a modern tent that erecting it takes barely five minutes, the thermal bed mat is self-inflating (an absolute godsend after all the puff that has been exerted during the day), the down-filled sleeping bag is snug and comforting, and the addition of the stolen pillow the perfect final touch.

In France I had often been the only person on the site, but things changed as I travelled east. The tiny tent and loaded bicycle never failed to attract attention which resulted in invitations to caravans where food and drink were always part of the deal. The most spectacular site was perched on the side of the Black Mountains overlooking a green valley. In spite of the weather's best efforts to spoil the occasion, the owner had welcomed me with wine, coffee and pretzels – all free of charge. I was the first in his visitors book for 2000. In horrible contrast to this, was a huge and packed site on the outskirts of Donaueschurung. It had the appearance of an out-of-town run down housing estate and it seemed that the caravans were permanent homes. The residents wore shell suits and the dawn chorus of guttural coughing was in sharp contrast to the normal bird song.

The sites were always good value and the only real variable was the quality of the showers. The end of day shower had taken on absurd importance in my routine; it had a therapeutic as well as cleansing quality. The French showers were free and delivered a trickle of luke warm water prompted either by pressing the knob in or worse by far, hanging on to a piece of string, which left only one hand free. Mastering the art of a thorough wash including hair was a challenge and any idea of shaving legs out of the question. Things improved dramatically in Germany and Austria. Never expensive and often free, the showers cascaded hot water. Paying for a decent shower never bothered me. The problem lay in the token which controlled the time and it was this that was so unpredictable as the water would cut off without any warning. The trick was to ensure that when this happened you weren't covered in soap and shampoo. As my towel is the size of a large flannel, any thought of heading to the office to buy another token was a non-starter. This towel, one of the many gifts from thoughtful family and friends, is a modern miracle. Lacking only in size, it has the texture and qualities of a chamois leather making it extremely absorbent, it weighs nothing and takes up little space.

(My family and friends had been so thoughtful and generous before I left. Amongst the gifts were an extraordinary watch which includes an electro magnetic compass, a water purifier, sandals, Swiss army knife, head torch, light weight trousers, exercise trousers, light weight waterproof top, bandana, baseball cap, tiny leather bound note book, camera, two $10 notes, some of the cycling gear, the wallet of family photographs. When a friend told me she had bought me a universal plug, I reacted hesitantly knowing that there would not be any electric appliances amongst my luggage. If there was no place for a mirror there was certainly no place for a hair dryer. I hated to think that she had wasted her money. But no – the 'plug' turned out to be 'universal' in the sense that it fitted any bath, basin or sink! And, like the rest, it earned it's place in the luggage.)

The Danube provided the background for many of these nights, and it was in a busy modern site that the incident of the loo paper occurred. On checking in, the woman at the desk had adopted the unusual procedure of charging for each aspect of my presence separately: myself; the bicycle; the tent; the shower; and local tax to round it off. Wise now to the problem of tokens, I asked how long the shower lasted and was thrilled to learn eight minutes – a lifetime. However, none of the loos, ladies or men's, had any paper and in this pristine and well ordered place it seemed likely that this was not the result of negligence. When I asked the woman at reception to give me a supply, she informed me that campers were expected to provide their own. Digging deep in to my German vocabulary, I pointed out that this was a luxury for which there was no space on my bicycle. This prompted a lengthy discussion with her colleague and after much pointing at me, she disappeared briefly, returning with a tiny roll. Remembering the booking in procedure it seemed an odds-on bet that there would be a piece by piece charge for this. Instead, she extracted a promise that it should be given back in the morning and I was trusted to take the whole thing. My German ran out when it came to questioning the fact that the very modern shower and toilet facilities were equipped with those extra jumbo sized holders, capable of dispensing nineteen miles of paper.

On emerging from the tent at dawn, I was astonished to see two cyclists in the open in their sleeping bags. I just cannot imagine that as an acceptable option. For the relatively small amount of space and weight that the modern tent takes up, it is inconceivable to consider travelling without one. In spite of being so diminutive, it has two sections: one with the built-in ground sheet to sleep in, with space over for some luggage; and, partitioned off with a mosquito net, the other (about one third of the capacity) officially described as *'the vestibule'* where the bulk of the luggage can be housed. This means that, apart from securing Alchemy and remembering to put a plastic bag over that bum-wrecking saddle, The Team were together, dry and private. How do these men cope if it rains? It's a fair bet they weren't carrying any loo paper either, but they looked too sound asleep to appreciate the offer of the remainder of mine.

The whole camping ritual became fine tuned. Success depended on packing in such a way that the minimum amount of disturbance was created amongst the panniers. It was easy enough to hurl gear here and there on arrival, but packing it up again in the morning.... another matter. And without the luxury of a car to sling the odds and ends into, I had to get it right. The panniers' sides were not elastic and they were all full to absolute capacity, every item had its place and was squished to its minimum volume. (It is unbelievable just how much the amount of space a T-shirt will take up varies depending on how it is either folded or rolled.) There was no margin for error.

The biggest nuisance when packing up in the morning was the condensation on the inside of the tent. Short of ceasing to breath, I never found a way to prevent this. Mopping it up was difficult but it was time well invested. If it wasn't done, the damp tent was difficult to pack, took up more space and was noticeably heavier – all very unwelcome attributes. The clever ruse was to pitch it in a place that ensured it caught the morning sun, nature's tumble drier. I could be up, dressed, washed, packed and ready for take-off in forty minutes. This had been honed down to a meticulous routine which initially had taken over an hour.

The most meditative and privileged places were those solitary times away from official sites: the night of my birthday spent on the side of a hill at the edge of a vineyard under a cherry tree; before crossing into Hungary tucked away in a tranquil no-man's land because the country road had been closed; an isolated field alongside the Danube.

So far.... so good....

Top: Isolated field, Germany
Bottom: Ferry across Danube, Austria

Top: Birthday in vineyard, Hungary
Bottom: Pedestrians in Rumania

Top: RSA offices in Rawalpindi, Pakistan
Bottom: My "Sponsor" in Pakistan

Top: Injured Alchemy, India
Bottom: Driver asleep on Grand Trunk Road, India

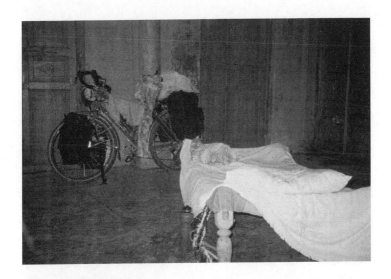

Top: Indian Temple
Bottom: Roadside topiary in Thailand

Top: Sightseeing truck, Thailand
Bottom: Elephants at work, Laos

ASIA

Chapter Nine

Having salvaged the disappointment in Turkey with a memorable cycling experience, it is time to fly to Pakistan. As direct flights are infrequent and fully booked I choose to ignore the travel agent's promise of a seat ('No problem, Pam') and travel via Bahrain and Abu Dhabi. Would Alchemy, my panniers and I all end up at Islamabad airport at the same time and undamaged?

While I am waiting there is plenty of opportunity to reflect on that moment when I spoke out loud for the first time those words 'I'm going to cycle around the world.' It was in a serious bike shop in Croydon where you had to ring a bell to gain entry (not the sort of place that sells fancy coloured lycra gear or puncture repair kits) and feeling very insecure, shy and embarrassed the sentence was spoken in a whisper. Would the man serving me burst out laughing or conceal a smirk of incredulity? At the very least retort *'Surely not at your age. Perhaps more sensible to join a lace making class.'*

But no, not even a titter.

'Excellent' Chas replied 'Where do you intend to go?'

This conversation cost me £1,685 and for the first time in my life I had my inside leg measured – not for a tailor made pair of trousers, but for a tailor made bike. It was time for my £60 second hand hybrid bike to have a rest.

I must have been the perfect customer because, knowing nothing about sprockets or any other part, all the specifications and details were left to the shop. The only contribution I made was when asked by Chas 'What colour do you want it to be?'

'Red' I said without hesitation. This was easy as both my first and last cars had been red.

'Believe it or not' he told me 'it can take some customers over an hour to make that decision.'

For the flight from Turkey to Pakistan Alchemy had to be reduced to several pieces in order to fit into a rather small bicycle box which had involved taking off wheels, mudguards, pedals and both racks. I was quite proud to have managed this all myself. Finally, several rolls of tape were wrapped around to secure everything.

It is now just after dawn at Islamabad airport and I feel very apprehensive waiting for the precious cargo to appear. Will it arrive at all? To have chosen a route involving two changes was inviting disaster. I am the last passenger in the baggage reclaim area and the sinking feeling in my stomach grows more intense, the anticipation unbearable. When the bike box finally appears, it is upside down on a trolley being pushed by a baggage handler and my relief on seeing it is instantly replaced with uncontrollable panic. The box has burst apart.... I start to tremble, feeling feint and sick. Hardly daring to approach for fear of what I might find in the shattered box, or more precisely fail to find, the temptation is to cower in a distant corner and start my nervous breakdown. Then, if possible, it gets worse. A lone mudguard rumbles into view on the luggage conveyor belt. What else might have fallen out (or been stolen): a wheel, a pedal, the front rack? This has all the makings of a catastrophe.

Dazed and distraught, I grab the mudguard, bundle my panniers onto the trolley and venture into the arrivals lounge. A recent rash of emails with RSA had indicated that accommodation might have been arranged as well as someone to meet me but nothing had been confirmed. The sight of the RSA logo held up by two men brings unimaginable relief and puts the panic attack on hold. Whatever the extent of my problems, at least there would now be local support and expertise.

'Miss Pam?' the older one enquires. 'I am Hamed, the office manager from Royal & Sun Alliance. Our main offices in Karachi have told us about your visit and asked me to collect you and your bicycle. The Karachi manager has a good friend here in Islamabad They used to be at college together and he has arranged for you to stay with his family. He is head of a bank and is looking forward to welcoming you.'

'Oh, Hamed, you will never know just how grateful and relieved I am to see you here this morning.'

'It is my pleasure to welcome you. I hope that you have had a good flight.'

'The flight has been fine but just take a look at the box. It's been shattered and I'm so scared that parts of the bike will have gone missing.'

'Shall we take a look now?'

'No' I reply, not daring to face the truth. 'Not here in the airport. I'll deal with it later.'

'This is Ahmir, the office boy. We have come in two cars as we wanted to be sure that we could fit everything in.'

'That is absolutely brilliant – it's so early and it's the weekend. Thank you so much.' Never were words of gratitude more genuine. Rescue again by two modern day knights, on their day off. I could have hugged and kissed him but sensed that this would have been beyond the bounds of local culture. What if they had fled?

The battered and jet weary Team is transported to a large and luxurious private home and met with kindness, English tea and juicy mangoes. What the house lacks in mod cons is made up for by servants, one of whom greets us – embarrassingly, I mistake him for the host. Putting the bruised Alchemy back together again proves a challenge, particularly as the two teenage sons insist on helping and their combined knowledge of bicycles is considerably less than mine. If the value of the specially made bicycle has not been appreciated before, this incident brings it home. Anything less robust would have been reduced to scrap metal after such treatment. It turns out that all that is missing are two water bottles, just about the only item which it should be possible to replace in Pakistan. It is nothing short of a miracle.

Sunday is spent with Hamed who takes me to Murree – a mountain resort set up by the British and used as a weekend getaway. This is my first experience of Pakistan traffic where driving on the correct side of the road appears to be an optional extra, whereas use of horn is obligatory. Anarchy reigns as the cavalcade of every shape and size of motorised vehicle, all belching out black exhaust fumes, weave their way amongst the non-motorised, including bicycles, rickshaws, carts drawn by anything with four legs. It seems doubtful that taking a driving test is part of the system but if it is, there could be only two reasons for failing: inadequate use of horn or driving with due courtesy and attention. There is a wonderful irony to what must result in frequent and fatal accidents. Many of the buses and trucks have black shrouds tied at the front and back – a symbol of protection.

And it has to be today of all days when diarrhoea strikes. Hamed has dedicated the whole day to entertaining me. The gurgling percolator which is now my stomach distracts dramatically from appreciating even the view, never mind coping with lunch and the pink Kashmir tea. The worst moment comes when my host insists that I sample the local favourite – barbecued corn on the cob. This is a form of roughage that would render the laxative counter of any Western chemist redundant.

During my stay the host family take me to the Islamabad Country Club. This establishment emphasises the chasm between the 'haves' and the 'have nots'. Lacking nothing and sumptuous in its facilities, there is no leisure pastime which is not catered for: bridge to swimming; hockey to squash; air conditioned restaurants and changing rooms. The teenage sons play tennis with friends and there are three ball boys in attendance. Their presence is taken as much for granted as the tennis net. Better than being poked up chimneys? Perhaps.

In the home there are servants for every chore: squatting on the lawn digging out individual weeds by hand; mowing the lawn with a mower that would be more in place at a car boot sale, if not the British museum; brushing carpets with dustpan and brush; hand washing all the family laundry; daily valeting of four cars; waiting at table; endless food preparation and washing up. They are on call seven days a week, twenty four hours a day, summoned with a yell. No smile, no please.

Typical of these encounters was a servant returning a gleaming pair of shoes to my host, Jamal. While the servant cowered, Jamal scowled during the prolonged period in which he intimately scrutinised the shoes (the shine of which no guards officer could have improved on). Jamal then turned abruptly and walked off. Eye contact? Thank you? Absolutely not. The servant slunk off. With massive unemployment and no social welfare, this form of abuse is easy to get away with. The servant who dares to venture *'Excuse me, did I hear please?'* or *'Didn't your mother teach you any manners?'* would be on the street before finishing the sentence. What is also unimaginable is that they have no privacy. They sleep on the floor (not the sofas or chairs) and presuming that they have a change of clothes, where that is kept is guesswork.

The only reason preventing me from setting off immediately is the need to obtain a visa for India. Hamed drops me at the Embassy in the naïve assumption that he could wait while the visa is issued. What catches me by surprise is that no containers (handbag, briefcase, carrier bag, rucksack) are allowed into the Visa Section and my tiny bum bag qualifies as such. There is no argument, though I do my best. After taking out my glasses, passport and US dollars (paradoxically all it contains) I barge back towards the entrance to give the now empty container to Hamed; not easy against the flood of incoming applicants, security guards, one way doors, iron railings and gates. Had he not chosen to hang on, it would be necessary to abort the venture till tomorrow.

There is the predictable wait but the queue has a semblance of order with an occasional surge of shoving and shouting when the security guards pounce and all goes quiet again.

The official behind the glass checks my details and says 'That will be 1,850 rupees.'

Having arrived on a Saturday morning and come straight to the Embassy first thing Monday, there has been no opportunity to visit a bank and until now all transactions for visas have been in dollars. Unconcerned I reply 'I haven't any rupees, but I've got plenty of US dollars.'

'That's no good here. I'm afraid I cannot accept dollars. It has to be rupees.' I am horrified. The implications are that the whole process will have to be started from scratch tomorrow but an Embassy is not the place to bargain or barter and my pleas go unheeded.

'You can borrow from someone' comes the apparently serious suggestion from behind the glass.

An idea strikes me. Turning to the queue stretched out behind I ask 'Would anyone be able to exchange dollars for rupees?' And so miraculously the problem is solved without even having to accept an extortionate exchange rate – another stroke of luck.

When handing my bum bag to Hamed we had agreed that he should go to the office and return four hours later to collect me. Six hours have now passed and there is still no sign of him. I am hanging around outside the Embassy and the heat is inescapable, even in the shade. The police become suspicious and ask me why I am loitering! The situation has great potential. I am carrying nothing but my glasses as the Embassy have retained my passport. I have absolutely no clue of either the name or address of my hosts, nor the location or phone number of the RSA office. What if he doesn't return? Of course he will, but what if…. And of course he does. It is impressive what two hours of mind games in vaporising temperatures can conjure up.

The Karachi manager feels that my presence as a guest in the home of his friend, the bank manager, should not exceed three days and as processing the visa is going to take five, it means moving to a hotel in Rawalpindi. The following observation might sound ungrateful but it is important to realise that this was a wealthy family with a battalion of servants and an entirely separate guest suite, so my stay is causing no disruption. It is the father, Jamal, who does not want me around. I am his worst nightmare – a liberated single woman who represents a threat to his control over the household. His wife and children are enjoying, in fact revelling in the diversion of having me in the house. They all speak fluent English and every one of them, apart from my host, has sought every opportunity to find time to talk to me.

The conversations with the teenage sons are never about my journey, focusing instead on the state of affairs in their country, with particular observations on relationships with India, the Kashmir problem and historical connections with England. Never any frivolous diversions about football and pop music. They are incredibly politically aware and articulate. The wife, her sister and his mother who also live in the house, have been keen to discuss more domestic aspects of life as women in Pakistan experience it. Many guests have been entertained in these three days, either friends or extended family, and they too delight in the opportunity to chat with a visitor from England.

Jamal, however, wanted none of it, to the point of rudeness by Western standards. He made sure that I was never invited into the central living room, so instead the guests would filter out and talk to me in the hall. If he came on this scene he would interrupt; if it was a guest he would guide them away; a member of his family would be sent on an errand. His wife and sons would never dare utter the words 'let her stay'. So, based on a quote of Winston Churchill that house guests are like fish and should be slung out after three days, I move on.

Chapter Ten

Cycling to Pindi is the first real continuation of my journey even if only sixteen miles but I am in Asia alone on a bike and I am very excited. A cheap hotel has been found to mark time till the visa comes through. Encouraged by the RSA office, I catch a bus to Taxilla where there are archaeological ruins some 5000 years old, discovered by the British. Once there, a motorbike rickshaw is the best way to cover the extensive area and as I step off the bus a crowd of the drivers gather around sensing a sucker. After much bartering which is handled by an English speaking student – 'no problem' he says (ominous echoes of my least favourite phrase) – a price of one hundred and fifty rupees (about £3) is agreed.

Less than one hundred yards into the journey I am concerned when the original driver swaps with another one amidst animated gesticulating and chattering. The next three hours are spent checking out three of the sites as well as the museum. This was the deal. But the driver has other ideas and it is his choice to visit to a dam several miles further out of town. Instinctively I have a bad feeling about this but because he speaks no English, all I can do is tap him regularly on the shoulder and point back in the direction of the town. There can be no misinterpreting my concern. I become convinced that he is using the opportunity to see it for himself as he makes several wrong turnings and has to consult locals for directions. When we finally arrive back at the town centre, all my misgivings are justified when he signals that I have to pay him five hundred rupees. With absolutely no intention of coughing up more than the agreed price, I shake my head and hands vigorously and he begins yelling at me. Within seconds a crowd of fellow rickshaw drivers are gathered to offer him support. There's an angry mood with a great deal of violent fist shaking and shouting.

Furious rather than frightened, I have the courage to yell above the noise 'Does anyone speak English?'

All the men in Pakistan wear *'shalwar kameez'* – resembling baggy cotton pyjamas – of various pastel shades, but even with this uniformity of clothing you can detect those with a bit more class and authority. Clean and ironed for starters. One such man approaches me. He turns out to be an off duty policeman with a modicum of English and on hearing my story produces a notebook and pencil and invites the driver and myself to the police station to settle the argument.

'Fine by me' I say, greatly relieved. My driver immediately if reluctantly agrees to accept the one hundred and fifty rupees.

My liberator then escorts me to the bus. 'I will wait with you until it leaves' he offers. 'Just in case there is more trouble.' So he does, and there isn't. There appears to be no end to the knights on hand to rescue me – on bicycles, in cars, at airports and in a crowd.

The bus charges me for two seats, a recognised practice for a woman travelling alone because no man will sit in the adjacent front seat – even if the woman is local. The difference in this instance is between ten and twenty rupees.

The *shalwar kameez* strikes me as the perfect gear for cycling in. It looks so cool and comfortable and something has to replace my shorts which would be unacceptable clothing for a woman in a Muslim country. But in spite of my very best efforts, no-one will sell the garment to me. During the coming weeks I discover that even men who wear a lounge suit and tie in the office change into the *shalwar kameez* in the evening. The only criticism I have is that when wearing them, men feel obliged to publicly and thoroughly scratch their dangly bits with uninhibited abandon.

During the three days at the hotel in Rawalpindi Riaz, the manager, shows extraordinary kindness but this develops quickly into obsessive and unwelcome attention. He wants to go for walks in the evening. He has invited me out for supper and brought food to my room. I am having to lock my door as he has taken to walking in without knocking. The initial friendly and helpful man has metamorphosised into morose and intrusive company.

'My life is a tragedy' Riaz told me. 'You are the only friend I have. I am so lonely.'

It is important to stress that my only role in this three day drama is as an attentive and sympathetic listener. Should I be surprised then to hear him utter those immortal words? 'My wife doesn't understand me.'

This is an altogether different landmark. To burst out laughing would be cruel but it is difficult not to. Could I really be hearing this? I have cycled half way around the world to hear the ultimate adulterous cliché spoken by a Pakistani husband.

On my last night he asks 'Can I spend the night in your room – just watching?' Yeah, right....

Even without an audience, I do not sleep well and find it easy to get up as intended at half past four. Riaz is there to bid me farewell but it is still dark so his tears will not be detectible. In any case there is no need for a tissue to wipe them away. With the temperature already 38°C they will soon evaporate.

It is pre-dawn and the reward for an early start is that it feels cooler! Just lying in bed with the overhead fan running flat out, sweat seeps from every pore and the effort of turning over is enough to step up the flow. Any real exertion such as cycling brings forth a deluge and within minutes my clothes are drenched. The Grand Trunk road, which crosses the entire breadth of Pakistan and India from Peshawar to Calcutta, is my route. In theory this would make it possible to dispense with a map for either country which could prove a blessing, as trying to buy anything in Pakistan which is related to India is futile. There is no imagining the feeling of mutual hatred.

European breakfasts have been replaced with mangoes which are in the height of their season. I am doing my best to prove that it is impossible to overdose on this delicious fruit but have still not found a way of eating them that does not require a second shower. (Three huge ripe mangoes cost forty pence.)

Of the three frightening incidents throughout the entire journey, two happen whilst eating. (The third was the attempted attack by those youths in Rumania trying to grab the bike.)

The first had been in Rumania while enjoying a picnic on a shady park bench in the town of Vinga when four gypsy women surrounded me, one sitting either side and two standing in front. They stared resentfully, then moving closer still, snatched at my clothes and demanded food, cigarettes and money. The need to rest and eat had to be abandoned so I shoved everything back in the carrier bag, hurriedly secured it to the back rack with the bungee chords and moved on. I was surprised at how distressed I had been made to feel by women.

It is during a breakfast of mangoes the other moment of anxiety occurs.

As a European woman in Pakistan and India you have to learn to cope with crowds gathering and staring, always passive and usually male. Only the flies are more intrusive and get closer. It is not intimidating but can be unnerving.

This morning has a different feel. Three men sit at my table and begin to talk to me. This is not the customary passive silence. Their gestures are hostile and threatening, indicating that they expect me to give them something. It is still early morning with nobody apart from the stall owner around. Dripping with mango juice, a quick escape is out of the question so I walk over to the tap to wash myself and the sticky Swiss army knife. My outward calmness does not reflect the quaking feeling surging around inside. They stick close to me and while one turns on the tap, another is insisting he hold the knife, indicating that it will be easier to wash my face without it. The ensuing tug of war denies any genuine good intentions. Still dripping, another hasty departure is necessary and their plan is thwarted.

(Looking back on the twenty countries which I travelled through, the thousands miles cycled and the almost daily warnings of danger, it is comforting to know that the reality is so different. Perhaps it was necessary to experience these three trivial moments of fear to understand my extreme good fortune the rest of the time.)

Feeling hugely chuffed to be on the road again, I am within ten miles of my destination when I am politely but firmly hijacked. A man riding a cranky old bike pedals alongside. On the back there are two crates of empty Pepsi bottles secured with rope.

His English is limited but that does not inhibit him. 'Come with me to my village' he invites. Looking precariously over his shoulder, wobbling and pointing behind he adds 'Nice cup of tea. Take only ten minutes.'

'No, I am sorry but I really cannot stop' I tell him.

He won't give up. 'I am also cyclist. I am soldier. I have wooden leg.' And to prove the point he hitches up his right trouser and there it is – a very primitive wooden leg.

The distance between us and the village increases as he repeats his invitation insisting always 'Only ten minutes. Just a cup of tea'.

Moments such as these are governed by instinct. As certain as I was that those gypsy women, teenage boys and breakfast intruders meant nothing but harm, this man's attitude and geniality persuade me at least to stop and think about his invitation, in spite of all those warnings about Pakistan being exceedingly dangerous and awash with fundamentalists.

And so, we double back towards the village on the wrong side of the dual carriageway. This counts as normal practice, even for trucks and buses. More bizarre – a vehicle deliberately driving on the wrong side of the road will insist on his right of way by hooting persistently at the legal on coming traffic! The two carriageways are separated more often than not by a substantial concrete barrier, about three feet high and two feet wide and official gaps to allow crossing over are very few. In order not to miss out on potential business driving past on the far side, the owners of petrol stations and large road side eating places smash an opening in this barrier wide enough to let a truck do a U-turn.

The ten minute tea break extends into four of the most extraordinary days of my journey. The village is a maze of narrow passages barely wide enough for a bicycle. There are only women and children in evidence. Abdul leads me to his primitive shop, the front room of his sister's house. No sign of shelves or a till – just a few boxes of vegetables on the floor and a selection of loose sweets. He was on a twenty mile round trip to the nearest town to replace the Pepsi when he overtook me.

Word spread quickly about an unusual visitor and for three hours an endless stream of women and children come to investigate. The children unabashed and excited romp around the room like puppies, giggling, pointing and trying to touch me. When Abdul isn't using his *'chadar'* (an extremely long cotton scarf) to mop the sweat from his skinny face, he uses it to swat them away. Those who can't get inside the small room hang from the bars on the window or stand on each other's shoulders to peer in.

The reaction of the woman could not be in more dramatic contrast. Very reserved, they arrive in ones or twos and stand placidly in front of me, gazing. Wearing full sari with just the face showing, they shake hands – just. It feels like holding a empty glove, limp and unresponsive. Many bring spicy naan bread, piping hot from the oven. These villagers have never experienced any other nationality in their midst, never mind an older Western woman travelling alone on a bicycle. It is as if I have indeed arrived from Planet Zog.

This presents a unique Kodak moment but as unworldly as they might be the whole bunch, women and children, instantly scatter at the sight of the camera.

Being the undiluted centre of attention proves overwhelming, most particularly because the only means of communication is sign language. Predictably, the first question is 'How old are you?' Even in sign language this is impossible to misinterpret. Their reaction is incredulity.

During this time it became clear that I represented a major coup for my friend with the wooden leg and he is very reluctant to let me go. Lunch at his home is next on the agenda where his wife has prepared a feast of several dishes just for me. As I would discover on future occasions, these situations demand that the guest eats alone, while the family looks on. Already full of naan bread and finding the spicy food way beyond my tolerance level, the situation if not the food is delicate and difficult to handle. And if the food is hot, it is nothing compared to the afternoon temperature which does little to entice an appetite. As I struggle to do justice to the spread, the shopkeeper, his wife and seven children sit around the room and watch me. They then insist I take *'aram'* (rest – a Pakistan and Indian favourite pastime, sometimes fulltime pastime which makes a Spanish siesta look like a power nap). I am expected lie down on a *'charpai'* (a wooden framed seat without a back and about the length of a bed) in this same room and sleep, as the family continues to stare.

Abdul is determined that I should stay overnight but with the saturation level of attention and very limited communication, I feel a strong need to move on. An unexpected compromise is reached. Anil, a man from the village, had moved with his family to Burnley, outside Manchester, thirty years ago and he returns every summer for a six weeks' stay. Just outside the village he is overseeing the building of two vast and luxurious houses, one for him and one for his brother, and he invites me to drop in for a chat. These palatial homes are a strong indication that his teacher's salary stretches a very long way when exchanged for rupees and building materials. Within the distance of less than a mile, I move from a medieval village to twentieth century luxury. I find myself sitting amongst a gang of builders and a Pakistani teacher with a strong Lancashire accent. He acts as interpreter and because there is a power cut (a several times a day occurrence), there is plenty of time to get beyond the matter of my age. As on building sites the world over, the kettle is put on (thanks to a gas cylinder) and tea brewed.

So, The Team's story unfolds and the men become more and more wide eyed.

As Anil points out 'These men would even not let their wives cycle to the next village'.

On his recommendation I check in to a hotel five miles down the road run by a friend of his who coincidently lives in Burnley as well. He also happens to be visiting and lets me stay two of the next three nights free of charge. The day ends with a trip to the Mangla dam, something all the locals are very proud of. They claim it is the biggest in the world. I wouldn't know about that but at least it is full of water, unlike its empty neighbour at Taxilla which had barely enough water to support a goldfish. The real highlight is getting there on a local bus; the sort where people hang out of the windows and cling on to the roof, and the hand luggage could vary from a bird in a cage to a full grown pig. The conductor runs alongside exhorting pedestrians to board amidst much shouting and banging on the side of the bus. It isn't unusual for passengers to jump on or off whilst the bus is still moving. The highway signs warning of road humps strike me as irrelevant as these are outnumbered by hundreds of substantial potholes, a far more effective way of slowing down any vehicle.

The following day is spent in the home of another of Abdul's sisters. This family lives in the town of Dina and two of the teenage children speak good English. Burnley is again represented, this time in the form of a teenage girl cousin, there much against her will for the whole of the summer holidays. The entire day is taken up with talking, eating, drinking tea and resting.

Towards the end of the day, Naeem, acting as interpreter, extends an invitation from his mother. 'She would like you to stay with our family for a month.'

'This is really very kind of her' I reply 'but I can't. Please thank her and say I am so sorry, but I must keep going.'

'Please, then, just a week.' It seems churlish to refuse but apart from using up precious days on my visa, there is real concern about how each day would be spent. There is a limit as to how much talking, eating, tea drinking and resting one could cope with.

The quality of life of such women is beyond anything imaginable in the West. There had been a strong indication that those women in the village never ventured out of it, unless it was to go to a nearby lake to wash clothes. The women in the town seemed not even to leave their home. The town is large and bustling with hundreds of street stalls and small shops, but never a woman to be seen. In the house where I am a guest, it is the husband or sons who do the food shopping. What else to do but rest? The daughter is responsible for cooking breakfast; the mother cooks the lunch and supper. Otherwise, nothing.

Her husband is retired from the army and commandeers the room with the television where he sits, or more precisely lies most of the time watching such diversions as *Who wants to be a Millionaire* Pakistan style. (Every country has its version of this programme. Identical in format, all that is missing is Chris Tarrant. And just how inflated must the title be in some countries, especially Turkey where one million lire is equal to £1.)

The house is large with several rooms on two floors surrounding a courtyard. No doubt a well-to-do family. But imagine the life of this woman. Not a single personal diversion: no hobbies, no gardening, no magazines, no local library, no cinema or theatre, no Starbucks, no aerobic or yoga class, never mind being let loose in a shopping mall with a credit card. Rest is what they do.

The concept of cycling around the world is beyond the mother's understanding. When she realises that my destination in Pakistan is Lahore her comment, passed on by the her son, is 'There is a train which goes to Lahore. You and the bicycle could travel on board in comfort and be there in a matter of hours.' If I fail to understand her life, how could I possibly expect her to understand what I have chosen to do? Never mind at my age!

The young cousin from Burnley seeks me out to explain her dilemma and ask advice. She was born and brought up in England, going to the local school and now at college. She has a boy friend and is in love. The fact that the lad himself is a Pakistani is not good enough. She dare not tell her parents as they have other ideas. An arranged marriage is the name of the game, both in Pakistan and India and there is a cousin (it seems always to be a cousin) lined up for her. It is one of the sons in the house where I now find myself. This chap has little education and speaks not a single word of English. The chasm between the cultures in which they have each been brought up is immense. There seems to be a huge element of injustice as far as this young girl is concerned. The expectation to abide by her parents wishes strikes me as unreasonable but not to do so would jeopardise her relationship with them. She loves and respects them and is keen to do the right thing.

'I am the eldest daughter; the favourite of my father. He expects me to obey him and I dare not even hint at the idea of choosing my own husband. I think that my mother might understand, but she would never take my side against my father. What do you think I should do?'

This is not a question that even the most seasoned agony aunt would want to involve herself with. We talk for hours but ultimately there is no compromise for her. It is with a horrified fascination that I watch as the intended engaged couple spend time in the same room. He is oblivious of any problem and she is distraught, totally ignoring him and refusing to make eye contact. It has been an upsetting experience.

The fourth day brings the climax of my stay – a visit to an ancient Mogul fort. This is my sort of sightseeing. The place is a World Heritage Site but is so remote and neglected that nobody visits it, unlike those ruins in Turkey where one is constantly jostling with huge crowds. During the entire day at the fort the only other living creature we see, apart from the few people who live there, is an iguana. Startled by the noise of the engine, it leaps out of a bush and runs faster even than the motorbike is travelling. It is the colour of sand and at least four feet long – a five star addition to my wild life inventory.

This day is very special. First a white knuckle ride on the back of a motorbike, driven by Naeem across fields, through rivers, up steep banks, slipping and sliding in deep sand and bumping over tracks consisting of rocks and boulders. A scramble course of some eight or nine miles where I (who boasts that no fair ground ride is too frightening) sometimes hardly dare to look over his shoulder. His skills as a driver are remarkable. To negotiate such treacherous territory on his own would be impressive, but with a passenger is quite incredible. Once in the fort we abandon the bike on several occasions to make long forays into the ruins. This young man played hide and seek in these ancient buildings during his childhood and knows the place intimately. There is much clambering and scrambling and at one point he encourages me to follow him across a very high and crumbling wall, with significant gaps which have to be negotiated (for this read *'leapt across'*). We spend hours exploring without mishap but it does strike me just how idiotic it would be to end up with a broken leg as a result of a sight seeing expedition.

'You are very strong' Naeem comments. This might be interpreted as 'I've never before seen a woman behaving in such a way'. He has already told me how shocking my short hair is in a country where all women wear their hair loose and hanging way below their shoulders. I ask him if either his mother or his sister have ridden pillion on his bike. 'No, neither of them have ever been on my motorbike. Not even in the town' is the reply.

Now it is time to move on and my concern is that at half past four in the morning all the hotel doors will be locked and my departure delayed. But no, even at this early hour the staff are up and take over with great enthusiasm and much smiling. All my luggage is carried downstairs, one of men fetches and holds Alchemy while I attach the panniers, another fills the water bottles, the doors and gates are opened and held back. Abdul has ridden the five miles in from his village to see me off. And finally a ceremonial waving goodbye. Life could not be better. Cooler maybe, but not better.

Chapter Eleven

The next town, Gujranwala, is dusty, smelly and disgusting – with the unenviable reputation of being the dirtiest place in Asia. All the evidence from Alchemy's saddle would not argue with this. Plus staggering volumes of traffic. Crossing and re-crossing the dual carriageway to check hotels, which have the knack of always being on the opposite side of the road, could seriously shorten your life. Just after noon, having covered seventy five miles, I book into a room at a cost of £4.50 (seems to be the going rate) and collapse on the grubby bed to be attacked by two new variations of blood suckers; fleas and what appear to be giant greenflies which inflict a nasty bite. At least, unlike the always present but invisible mosquitoes, there is a chance of swatting this lot.

'Be grateful' the hotel manager observes. 'At least there are no mice.'

Waking up next morning it is impossible to prize my eyelids apart. This is not tiredness or conjunctivitis; just the consequence of all the accumulated dust from my previous day's ride. Contact lenses, for all the freedom from the nuisance of glasses that they bring, would never be an option in these parts. My departure, again around four thirty, has the added excitement of carrying all my gear down four flights of stairs in the dark. This is not due to an electricity cut – there are no bulbs in any of the lights. This time no help is offered by a surly couple of young men on night duty.

Yesterday evening they persuaded me to leave the water bottles in the fridge over night so they would be cool for the journey. This fridge was behind the bar in the restaurant and I knew it was risky, worried they would still be there in the morning. And frankly the idea of chilling water is farcical. The heat is such that within minutes of being attached to the bike, the water could almost burn your tongue. Was it possible to become paranoid about a few litres of water? Definitely – I have become a waterholic. Whatever its temperature, it represents survival.

However, their intention had been thoughtful, so it seemed ungrateful not to play along, only to find my worst fears justified. The three bike bottles have been drained and are empty and my cache of three two litre bottles of water (which I am now having to buy) has vanished. I am absolutely furious, almost hysterical with rage. It is pre-dawn – what will be the chances of replacing them? Water from the tap is out of the question and the idea of setting off without any liquid is verging on suicidal. In the circumstances it seems more than justified to help myself to two cans of Seven Up – a token replacement. This, more than the dark stairs, nearly causes my downfall. In spite of the signed receipt which I produce, the hovering staff are not even convinced that the hotel bill has been paid. As they speak no English any explanation is futile. There is only one solution – make a quick but not so easy getaway. With both men grabbing at my T-shirt and me shoving them away, I climb on the bike and pedal off into the dusty dawn, my legs trembling and my heart thumping. It does not seem like a good idea to look over my shoulder to see if they are giving chase. Fear of dehydration has turned me into a thief....

And so on to Lahore, described by all tourist books as a dangerous city. Money and valuables such as cameras regularly get stolen from hotel rooms in the backpacker area of the town. Even the safes aren't safe. During the first hour of my ride a group of men at one of the hundreds of roadside cafés beckon me to join them. This fits in perfectly with my timetable of needing chai and something to eat so I pull off the road. One of them owns a calor gas business (outside which is parked an expensive car), as well as this adjoining café, and his servants are preparing the food for the day so there is much chopping and peeling going on. One of the questions that regularly crops up is about sponsorship (further down the list than that one about age) and there is always surprise at learning that I am funding the journey myself. It turns out that this chap is keen to become a sponsor! It comes to no more than two free cups of tea and a bun.... But, it's a start.

It does become shockingly obvious as I journey on through Pakistan and India that there is a sponsorship war being waged between Coca Cola and Pepsi. The evidence is clearest at the thousands of roadside eating places. Amongst the drab and impoverished surroundings, these cafés stand out in the glaring red or blue of the appropriate company – a complete make-over with sponsor's logo painted with pristine white background on walls and roof, visible from every angle, banners draped everywhere and the plastic tables and chairs reinforcing the message – everything either red for Coca Cola or blue for Pepsi.

It reminds me of cycling in the High Atlas mountains in Morocco. Needing water (which would be purified with iodine tablets) the group had stopped in the clichéd, but entirely accurate, middle of nowhere where a man carrying two buckets was lowered into a sixty foot well. Amongst the homes, which looked more like giant sandcastles, was a ramshackle stall with huge Coca Cola logos plastered all over it. Fresh pure water – none. Carbonated caffeine – plenty.

This battle for corporate loyalty turns out to be high profile for the remainder of the journey. In China the protagonists are McDonalds and KFC, always placed strategically next to or opposite each other. The battleground changes in Mexico. The names of ranches are displayed at the pillars of the gate on a large board – supplied by Coca Cola or breweries. And it is the company name and logo which are dominant; the name of the ranch almost irrelevant.

And talking of the power of a logo, once again RSA are expecting me and it is impossible to describe the thrill and relief I feel at the sight of the company symbol. Finding the offices has meant navigating miles of suburban streets, busier than I imagined possible. The seething swarm of humanity is made up of bicycles, which are in the majority, carts, mopeds, scooters, motorbikes, rickshaws, buses, cars, trucks. Everything on the move. Controlling this mayhem are policemen, immaculately turned out in white uniforms. They work in twos, standing on raised platforms in the centre of crossroads, holding each other's hand as well as an umbrella. The sun is up there in a cloudless sky but completely shielded by the dust and exhaust fumes which saturate the air. (My tan disappears in the following months. It seems that pollution is an effective sunblock.)

In spite of the shower earlier this morning, my physical state on arrival is similar to that of Lahore – smelly, dusty and disgusting. The manager, Shahbaz, seems unfazed and we talk while I demolish several large glasses of iced water and two steaming mugs of tea.

'What is your budget for hotels?' he asks.

My intention is to stay at the YMCA, the only place reputed to be safe, so without hesitation I reply 'I haven't had to pay more than £4.50, so hopefully something in that region, although I appreciate that city prices might be a bit more.'

He is unable to conceal his look of astonishment, disbelief and pity.

After phoning home he extends an invitation. 'My mother and my wife insist that you should stay with us in our small and humble home.' (Somehow the words *'small'* and *'humble'* don't ring true and it turns out that the house is anything but, unless compared with a Mogul fort.)

He arranges for his car and driver to collect me and my status experiences a dramatic change. I am treated as an honoured guest, allowed to do nothing, least of all push Alchemy or carry my panniers. I am brought breakfast in bed and the bed is made once I have got up. Referred to as *'Memsahib'*, an umbrella is held over me when standing in the sun or rain. Sightseeing is done from the back of a chauffeur driven car and if I choose to visit a garden or museum, the driver waits for me. During my absence he definitely gains standing amongst his peers because of his weird passenger. A huge and attentive crowd has always gathered around him by the time I return, to be greeted with a great deal of pointing, grinning and gesticulating.

Shahbaz' wife, Meera, is also Pakistani but was born and educated in the States. However, her current lifestyle gives no clue of this. She has adopted the full Pakistan wife role, subordinate to her mother-in-law with no control and no diversion. She is honest enough to admit that, in spite of all the would-be myths about arranged marriages and the *'happy ever after'*, affairs and adultery are rife in the city. Her mother-in-law does nothing but complain about her health and the problems she has with running the house. What – too many servants, or not enough? Nice problem.

Once in his house, Shahbaz completely ignores me and always communicates with his family (who all speak fluent English) in Urdu. His father on the other hand turns it on when it suits. Khalid has an ego larger than his two Mercedes and is full of promises: interviews with press and television, visits to his club, his farm ('No problem' he assures me....) none of which materialises.

He unwittingly sums up the family scene when he says 'It has taken a long time, but I have finally managed to convert my wife into behaving like my mother.'

The evening before my planned departure I discover Alchemy's back tyre has a puncture. I am about to put my theoretical knowledge to the practical test when Shahbaz and Khalid step in – not by rolling up their sleeves and fixing it, but by telling the chauffeur to drive the bicycle to a bicycle repair shop where for 10p the job is expertly done! This is the second occasion which proves the *'man's work'* theme, albeit with a different slant. Whatever it takes, I'm not complaining.

My plan is to cycle to the Indian border but this is sabotaged as Khalid will have none of it. With his own agenda and complete disregard for my preference, he insists that the only safe way is in the car, so the fifteen miles are covered with Alchemy ceremoniously perched in the back of a Mercedes with a CD plate and that is how we arrive at the Customs House. This comical entourage does my cause no harm. Six backpackers are crossing at the same time and the Pakistan customs officers are sifting meticulously through every item in their luggage. As they are leaving the country one wonders why they are receiving such intrusive attention. This might have something to do with the fact that, as this is the only road crossing for thousands of miles and seldom used, the job's worth type of official revels in the occasional opportunities that come his way. Anyway, The Team pedals straight through, passing at least five officials on either side of the border and having to show my passport on every occasion.

Whereas the Pakistan officers were weighed down with uniform and guns, those on the Indian side are impossible to identify. A voice hails me from a group playing cards at a table in the shade. It comes from the only one in something vaguely resembling a uniform and he wants to see the passport. Another, without a uniform but wearing a very impressive turban, demands that he looks at the passport. Perhaps just a curious bystander? In the Customs Hall they are playing table tennis and one officer offers me his chai while he goes for a spin on Alchemy. It is hard to conceal my laughter as he struggles not to fall off. His colleagues each take their turn with an equally spectacular lack of success.

I have managed to buy a map of India on the Pakistan side. Even with the knowledge that the GT road would lead all the way to Calcutta, it is inconceivable that the journey should be tackled on a day to day basis without more specific details. And, I cannot imagine life without my daily fix of scrutinising the route. The second hand trading of maps and travel books at the border fell into the gold mine category. The stall owner offered me three choices but the normal option of bargaining was not to be. He had one price and it was 'Pay up or use your compass'.

Chapter Twelve

Once in India, there is an immediate transformation. There are crops growing on either side of the road; women appear on bicycles and more surprisingly driving motorbikes and scooters, with women pillion passengers, many wearing western clothes. Amritsar is the first night stop and also the next sightseeing opportunity, a must – The Golden Temple.

Temples in India, even one as renowned and busy as this, offer travellers the opportunity to sleep the night and I have been very excited at this prospect. But sadly the bicycle is banned, so it is my first experience of an Indian hotel. The fan in the room is not the normal ceiling affair, but one attached to the wall, similar to those more usually situated on desks. It is fixed in one position pointing straight at the bed and has two speeds: flat out and supersonic. Clothes and paper take to the air, but to turn it off risks drowning in perspiration. Trying to sleep in this simulated wind tunnel proves impossible but there are compensations. The gale prevents the mosquitoes from landing to feast. However, there is an infestation of ants and spiders on the floor, so walking barefoot is not an option. Once again, it is a relief to get up at half past four.

The GT road is straight, straight and straight as well as flat, flat and flat, with an excellent surface. Ideal for cycling, in theory. But with temperatures in the roaring forties combined with extreme humidity, suddenly even sixty miles becomes a challenge. Searching for shade and food, an unusually smart restaurant appears – more the appearance of a country club, with high walls and an extremely large garden scattered with tables and umbrellas. Encouraged by the sign 'Fast Foods' I head towards the entrance but one of the armed guards blocks my way and without a word makes it clear that the bicycle would have to remain on the outside. Not just absurd (the garden is huge with dozens of empty tables) but not an option for me to leave the bicycle and my possessions out of sight on the busy public pavement. Equally without a word I insist on bringing the bicycle in. By now all his colleagues have gathered around sensibly pointing out that, whatever the Rule Book demands, in this instance nobody was going to object. Job's Worth will have none of it and continues to threaten me, to the extent of pointing to his gun! 'Yeah, big boy' I mutter. *'Small dick'* would have been more satisfying but imprudent. Finally, persuaded by his colleagues, a compromise is reached whereby Alchemy is propped against the wall just inside the gate. An entirely unnecessary drama.

The trucks defy physics as they are always grossly overloaded and lean at impossible angles. To find them broken down or having veered off the road is a frequent sight. I come across the most outstanding example at six o'clock one morning. The truck has overturned on a dual carriageway, spilling its load of full sacks everywhere. The driver is sound asleep on his bed mat in the middle of the road in front of his capsized lorry and absolutely oblivious of his surroundings. (This is the Grand Trunk road – the equivalent of the A1 in England.)

The side of the road brings a less welcome feature. Early in the morning it serves as the communal public lavatory for any nearby village. The sure sign is dozens of men, women and children walking along the verge carrying a bottle of water. Having selected their individual spot, they squat with their backs towards the road – mass and uninhibited mooning. Several miles of my morning ride would be lined with bare bums.

Phagwara, the destination for the day, is reached by noon and desperately thirsty I demolish a cold beer while checking into a hotel – this is the first alcohol since Hungary. It costs fifty five rupees, half the price of my room for the night and the equivalent of several substantial meals, but it hits the spot.

After collapsing and dozing for three hours, too exhausted to worry about the lack of water in the shower, I venture into the town. Staying in a hotel takes away any opportunity to meet local people, and besides I need to buy fruit for tomorrow.

Once again my life is taken over by a stranger, Steve, who interrupts my purchase.

'I was worried that the stall owner would charge you too much. We are not used to tourists here and it is a great temptation.'

'That's very kind of you' I say in appreciation, and then add 'Would you be able to tell me where I could go and have chai. It will give me a chance to sit and take in my surroundings. Also I've cycled miles today and am still very thirsty.'

This conversation leads to an extraordinary four days, as Steve persuades me not to leave in the morning. He has a brother, Goldie and between them and their father, Mohammed, they run several shops in Phagwara, one of which sells stainless steel cooking utensils; another supplying building materials. This family lives a great distance from the poverty line (but all in the same house) and between the three men a full agenda is drawn up for me.

Both brothers are officiating at a cousin's wedding to which I have been invited. The entire celebration centres on the groom who arrives several hours before his bride. Utterly stunning, dressed in scarlet and dripping with gold, she looks the picture of misery. So beautiful and so melancholy, she is unable to make eye contact with anyone but her mother. Even in the presence of videos and cameras she cannot raise the slightest smile. Her husband has fixed an agonising permanent smile on his lips, while his knuckles are white as his hands clench the arms of his throne. It is the second time that the couple have met, the first occasion being the engagement ring ceremony three months earlier.

I had been included in such a ceremony of another couple the previous day which ran along similar lines. The girl was almost an afterthought. None of the ritual chanting and incense burning served as an interruption to guests devouring of food. Initially a conveyor belt of waiters cruised around with trays of sweet and savoury temptations, with an equal number carrying trays of drink – all non-alcoholic. After these appetisers, the buffet proper kicked in, with the tables buckling under the choices. The music competed to be heard above the sound of the several jumbo sized air conditioning units which were failing to cool the marquee.

The third morning Steve collects me at seven o'clock (never did I believe that this would represent a lie in for me) and we drive to a truly private health club. The brothers had formed a syndicate with several others and built an exclusive facility which includes swimming pool, sauna and steam room (a somewhat unnecessary extravagance in a country which is one giant sauna and steam room), fully equipped gym, air conditioned lounge, all maintained by a servant who doubles up as cook, cleaner, gardener, driver, car valet, open gates, fetch papers and, for good measure, personal masseur. This brings about my second massage of the journey, the difference being that the poor man has obviously never worked on a woman before, never mind a European. He is petrified and has to be dragged to my (fully clothed) body where he spends a long time concentrating on my feet! I make the mistake of complimenting him on the strength in his hands, when he becomes much more bold and my body becomes the victim of Chinese burns and a pummelling that leaves bruises. The morning ends over breakfast and Sunday papers, in both Hindu and English, in the company of six turbaned Sikhs.

It has become clear that I represent a big catch for the men in this family, as more functions are laid on. The brothers even pay for the extra days in my hotel and tell the manager to ensure that the water in the shower is sorted. Some rewarding and relaxing hours are spent in the father's stainless steel emporium, perched on a cushion and fed endless drinks and food while all his customers are paraded in front of me, grinning and shaking my hand.

There is a worrying poster on display in this shop. *Just how special can you make a woman feel?'* And what is it advertising? A pressure cooker.

'I have arranged for you to have two interviews with the press' Steve has proudly informed me. 'One is from the local paper and the other is the Punjab Times.'

Perhaps this would be my fifteen minutes of fame. The first interview is conducted in a shop selling car tyres, because this is where the journalist is employed in his day job. Speaking fluent English, he skips past all the fundamental issues that interest everybody. Even my age seems of little consequence.

Within a couple of minutes, pen at the ready he asks 'Are you on a peace mission?'

'Good heavens, no. I'm on a bike ride.'

'Don't you want peace in the world?' he continues in an accusing tone.

'Of course I do. Everybody wants peace.'

'So, you are on a peace mission. You are riding around the world to bring the message of peace to all the countries you travel through.' (He hasn't even bothered to ask which those are.)

'No – I've told you. Mine is a personal journey with no purpose other than to cycle further each day until I finally get back to England. I am not trying to make any statements, but I understand that peace is important.'

'So, this is a peace mission, then.'

His persistence and stupidity bring a far from peaceful reaction from me. Alchemy has chosen today to have its third flat tyre and I could cheerfully strangle him with the punctured inner tube.

The second interview is worse. Grossly overweight, this man sits sweating profusely, again choosing to ignore even my age, and incredibly launches in to the peace mantra.

I repeat the denials, only to hear him continue 'So, you are doing this for nuclear disarmament throughout the world.'

All my patience and interest in humouring him vanish at this moment. If this is what my fifteen minutes of fame demands, then anonymity seems the preferable option. Steve, however, makes sure the photographer earns his keep. He manoeuvres things so that several photos are taken of the two of us outside one of his shops!

On the last day Mohammed invites me back to his house. Up until now the three wives have ignored me but on this afternoon, sharing guavas still warm from the tree, Steve's wife chooses to share some of her thoughts with me. As the wife of the older son, she has obligations. She lives in her in-laws' house along with her other sister-in-law and is utterly fed up sharing duties with two other women. With the mother-in-law ruling the roost, she has little control and all she wants to do is go out to work, but this is considered improper. The only time that her eyes truly light up is when reminiscing about a trip that she and her college friends had made to south India as a group on their own. Freedom, but only on that single occasion.

Mohammed is a small, skinny man, with a couple of front teeth missing and always barefoot. Unlike his sons who wear western trousers and shirts, he wears the traditional white cotton two piece outfit. It is difficult to associate him with his huge and magnificent home. Since my arrival he has been keen for me to stay there (for a month) but the wives vetoed the idea. This evening, just he and I sit at the large polished wooden table while the three wives prepare our meal. The two of us eat together and they eat in the kitchen. During the meal Goldie returns, collects his food, walks through the dining room to his bedroom without a word and shuts the door. (He is aware that I am leaving early tomorrow morning and hasn't said goodbye.) I am getting used to this all or nothing treatment – it has been consistent since my arrival in Pakistan.

My smiling toothless friend drives me back to the hotel where, at the entrance, I shake his hand and without thinking gave him peck on the cheek. He really has been so generous and thoughtful and unlike treatment from his sons, where I was prone to become invisible if not needed, he has been consistent in his kindness and attention. He withdraws as if about to be infected with a terminal disease, exclaiming 'ne ne' and leaving me feeling deeply embarrassed for getting it wrong. Then, ignoring my protests, he insists on accompanying me upstairs to my room. He follows, shuts the door.... and then grabs me. No subtlety or pre-amble about a lack of understanding from his wife and it is definitely my turn to say 'ne ne'. This does the trick whereupon he shakes my hand with an *'it was worth a try'* toothless grin and leaves.

Less than five minutes later there is a knock on the door. Surely not Mohammed back. But no, having completely ignored me all day, Steve has sent his driver at ten o'clock in the evening to fetch me over to his club for a night cap. Not the health club but a drinking and dining club, strictly men only – but exceptions can obviously made for a female when she is a temporary member of Steve's trophy cabinet. All the men are hitting the hard stuff very hard (whisky the alcohol of choice) and scoffing plates full of food. Those present are upset at my pronouncement that I am extremely relieved not to have been born an Indian wife.

Chapter Thirteen

The time has come to pedal onwards. During one of my many banana and chai stops, I have a very Indian experience. Sitting at a table by myself, apart from six million flies – swatting at them is a pointless waste of energy – a truck pulls up and I am astonished to watch about seventy people disembark, mostly men. (The back of the truck has been converted into a double-decker with a false bottom and there are also several hammocks.) Good business for the café owner one would think, but no. They use the water tank to wash and the tap to drink from and buy absolutely nothing.

Alchemy is propped up against a tree a short distance away. Half the group surrounds the bicycle; the other half surrounds me. The bicycle always attracts intense interest, most particularly because of the derailleur gears, the equivalent of space technology when it comes to cycling in India. They are all riding around on bikes which our grandparents would have been proud to own and with no evidence of lubricating oil. Apart from all the chatter, there is much prodding and poking amongst the bicycle's most private parts and I am beginning to feel a twinge of panic. Alchemy is completely shielded from me and a vivid picture is forming of the group continuing their journey leaving the bicycle stripped of everything except, if they have any sense, the Brooks saddle. The café owner can see my agitation and signals that all will be OK. He also refuses to take any money for my two glasses of chai. Those squatting very closely around me just stare passively. I had paid a comparative fortune for a tiny can of baked beans which are intended to provide much needed energy but trying to eat them in the close company of both eyes and flies proves more than I can cope with. It is time to go and I am about to pedal off when seventy voices are raised in unison. Are they jeering or saying goodbye? On turning around, it becomes evident that my mittens and cap are still on the table – the chorus was to let me know I had forgotten them.

The ride today is a killer – I am suffering from too much heat and too few calories. With still ten miles to go I spot a dusty lane with a morsel of shade. (There is no respite from this heat other than an air conditioned building. Shade, cloud or even night time bring no real relief; it is more debilitating than I can describe. Hot flushes surely never trouble menopausal women here as that is all life is – one long hot flush. Buffalos have the answer – they wallow in muddy ponds and I've been tempted many times to join them. Fantasies of waking up to a cold grey November's morning taunt me.) Carelessly slinging The Team on its side and grabbing two water bottles, I collapse in the dusty shade a few yards down the track. By now mugging, rape, even an arranged marriage would be preferable to any attempt at having to continue.

The last agonising ten miles end a gruelling eighty mile total for the day and my inquiries for a place to stay lead me to a Government rest house where there is no charge. The mattress and sheet seem to have been in place since the days of the Raj, bearing all the evidence of every possible bodily function and the showers are a shared facility. I wander into the town with another magical result. Plasters are on the shopping list, as I am discovering that cuts just do not heal in this heat and a couple are beginning to cause concern. The pharmacy is run by a doctor and before I know it, a tray of tea and cakes is produced – he is keen for me to stay and chat. Because this is also his surgery we are frequently interrupted by patients seeking treatment. Pills of every shade and shape are dispensed sparingly after a brief consultation. This might involve a stethoscope, the inspection of an ear using a torch and the naked eye, a tap on the chest and when the power fails for an hour, everything continues without a pause.

'This is India' he comments with a wry grin as he lights some candles.

His wife invites me to return later for supper where the food has been prepared specially for me. Once again, I eat alone while the doctor, his wife and one of their sons sit and watch. There are difficult moments as so much traditional Indian food is too spicy or sickly or scary for my taste buds and stomach, and with three sets of eyes fixed on you, there is no way of pretending. (I sincerely hope I did their kindness justice.) In my honour, the wife, also a Sikh, has put on her full regalia, turban and a large knife, almost a sword, all signifying a deep religious commitment. They invite me to stay overnight and have breakfast with them before leaving, but the four thirty deadline is top priority and I decline. A decision that is to haunt me for the next two days.

If it is possible to be rearing to go well before dawn, then that is the case. It is always a thrill to load up the bicycle and get under way and this morning is no different. Trying to get past, through, over, under a very shut level crossing proves challenging and after that it is head down with a determination to get as many miles under the wheels before the dreaded sun makes its unwelcome murky appearance. Making excellent progress using the drop handlebars (which significantly reduces wind resistance and increases speed) I have been travelling along a straight road with an excellent surface – nothing to look out for because it is still too early for much in the way of traffic. Curbs, pavements and lay-bys have not existed for hundreds of miles. Then, in the middle of nowhere, instead of the normal mud or gravel signifying a place to pull off, some lunatic has built a lay-by with a concrete curb eighteen inches high. It appears in my line of vision about six inches ahead of my front wheel and as my speed is nineteen miles per hour I have no time to swear or swerve, never mind brake. Result – blood pouring from my face, but much more worrying poor Alchemy caput big time. The impact has pushed the front fork back at least four inches and smashed the front rack which carries two panniers – disaster – and it is only just five o'clock.

The fact that it is entirely self inflicted makes it so much worse. It could have been avoided if only…. The strange thing is that there is no compulsion to disintegrate into tears of self pity. Far from hysterical, I realise that I am stranded – without a mobile. That hi-tech piece of equipment that one of my sons, Russell, was so keen for me to carry but I had stubbornly refused, confident that it would serve no purpose. Now, there is little comfort in proving the point. They would not have been happy to receive this phone call. The only immediate solution is to hitch a lift to…. well I could hardly be picky. This would have proved challenging enough in the familiar surroundings of south east England. There is little traffic but nevertheless, blood-stained and distraught, I wave my arm at anything that passes.

(The longer my journey continues, the stronger has become the feeling that I am not on my own in the spiritual sense. On hearing my stories many strangers have said to me 'You have a god' or 'There is somebody up there taking care of you' or 'God is on your side' or 'You are being protected' or 'The spirits are with you' or 'The universe is looking after you' or 'You have your own guide' – whatever form of wording they might choose. Every day I spend time meditating and drawing on that presence, expressing gratitude and seeking guidance, protection and help.)

It is barely dawn – will my guide be awake and on the case? Within half an hour a truck stops. Proving something of the truth about a picture painting a thousand words, both men climb down and without a single utterance to each other or to me, sum up the situation as quickly as it had taken me to create it. The injured bicycle is carefully handed up into the back of the truck, the panniers and my battered self into the cab. There is no fuss, no drama. The thirty mile drive to Ambala is carried out in complete silence. Amazingly, they not only don't speak to each other but show no curiosity about my situation. It was almost as if this was just another day for them. Happened all the time. Finding a bleeding western woman with a trashed bike on the side of the road at dawn – nothing unusual here. They don't even ask me my age.

Grateful for the lack of intrusion, I have time to formulate a plan. I thrive on spontaneity, flying by the seat of my pants but this is a stage too far.

My silent knights drop me off near the bus station in Ambala. Every corner in every town has a man squatting in front of a bowl full of water, an old inner tube and some glue, as well as a hammer. It is the local bicycle repair centre. This particular *'mister fix-it'* flinches at the sight of my mutilated bike. Amidst much tut-tutting and head wobbling, I have to hire a rickshaw to take The Team to the bus only three hundred yards away.

Never could the RSA connection prove so valuable. Even in my misery, it is possible to reflect on the irony. Eight years previously a secretarial agency had to persuade me, kicking and screaming, to undertake a month's contract in their Horsham offices. It was an environment that represented everything I loathed and despised. A human clone – definitely not for me. Having had the thrill and reward of running my own shop selling frozen food for twelve years (eventually shafted by the out-of-town supermarket), I had since struggled to find a satisfying way of earning a living. Age and experience were against me and lying about both had only thrown up a couple of unsuccessful interviews. When the RSA job was offered to me on a permanent basis, it posed a genuine dilemma – to trade my expectations and principles for a regular income. Common sense prevailed and so with a very bad attitude as well as untoward and excessive grumpiness, I accepted.

The bus arrives at the seething bus station in Delhi and all help evaporates. Hundreds of faces watch intensely as I clamber up the ladder on to the roof and struggle to get Alchemy down without inflicting further damage, trying desperately at the same time to keep an eye on my panniers which have been left on the pavement. When I indicate that I need a rickshaw, there is an instant change in mood and I am overwhelmed with offers of assistance, but realising how vulnerable I am, I take plenty of time to negotiate a deal. A journey to the RSA offices for one hundred rupees – the driver has bright orange hair, a popular trend with older men.

But the rickshaw is nowhere to be seen and to get to it entails walking up stairs, along passageways, across a bridge, down stairs, over a building site, through a rubbish dump carrying awkward and heavy gear – the bicycle (which cannot be wheeled because of its wound), as well as the panniers. The real nightmare has begun. As the bicycle has to be tied to the side of the motorised rickshaw, this vile, ghastly, cheating little monster then has to hunt through the rubbish to find something suitable for the task. The lopsided vehicle heads off into the bustling street and after several minutes the carrot topped bandit pulls into a petrol station and demands three hundred rupees from me – he needs to buy petrol and the price has trebled because of the difficulties imposed by the bicycle.

My calm demeanour is shattered by his aggression. Taking on the full victim role, I begin to shake uncontrollably and burst into tears. His question 'Why are you crying, lady?' makes me want to hit him – hard. Instead I curl up into a snivelling wreck and desperately keep my eye open searching for the comfort of that RSA logo. We arrive, but the scrawny little bastard has more tricks up his sleeve. He refuses to untie the bicycle until I hand over a further two hundred rupees and then has the audacity to suggest that he will be able to arrange my accommodation. I tell him that if it comes to needing his help to find a bed, then sleeping rough amongst the beggars on the street would be my preferred option.

As much as the manager and his secretary, Manjit, have been expecting me, they are not prepared for the apparition waiting in the foyer. My crash has left me with grazes on my forehead, nose and chin; my lips are swollen and there is rather too much evidence of a bleeding nose on my T-shirt. (Two spectacular black eyes will emerge in the next forty eight hours.) What happens during the next couple of days is nothing short of a miracle. My guide surely doesn't sleep – definitely a 24/7 individual.

Insurance was one of many items to tick off the list before leaving. With some difficulty a policy had been found to cover every aspect of my journey – except the bicycle. Even with my non existent expertise, I am aware that this repair will be way beyond the scope of a couple of hefty blows with a hammer, so without the powers of Yuri Geller, I have even been contemplating the idea of using a courier to return the bike to Chas Roberts to get it fixed.

But, if you have to trash a bike, then India is the country to choose. A nation of professional bodgers, Alchemy is restored to perfect health within twenty four hours for the cost of less than a pint of beer. The man who performs this astonishing feat of engineering even apologises that it comes to a few rupees more than his original quote. The front rack has been reduced to several pieces and needs the skills of a welder (whose workshop is the pavement and whose workbench is a piece of railway track). Squatting on his haunches, the job is completed in less then ten minutes for twenty pence and he assures me that it will be stronger than before – a theory which I fervently hope remains unproved.

Chapter Fourteen

Once again I am privileged to be amongst a family as Manjit extends an invitation to stay. She is married and lives with her husband's parents – customary practice. Being involved with such an extensive and wealthy household introduces me to experiences way beyond the normal traveller's domain. During this time not a single day passes without either a family birthday, or a national or regional festival.

One of the advantages of living in the home of a wealthy family is the air conditioning. Each room has its own unit (heading the list of gifts at the time of the wedding). But running them is expensive and so use is only encouraged while the room is occupied. The consistent hum of the motor is more than compensated for by the cool air making sleep much easier. The morning always arrives along with a raging thirst, but then this is nothing new to me.

Manjit has a responsible job in a global organisation and goes to work in Western clothes. However on returning home she is at the beck and call of her mother-in-law, who has told me 'I wanted her to give up work to be at home for me.' The compromise is that Manjit would sit with her on returning home. The only privacy Manjit has is in her bedroom with the door shut. The inside of the house is due to be repainted and during my visit the choice of colour has been the subject of much discussion. Manjit wants her bedroom painted plain white, but her mother-in-law prefers something else and so Manjit's preference is ignored. The Indian marriage does not so much reflect *'love me, love my dog'* as *'love me, love my entire family'* – but with luck at least some of them might live in Burnley.

Apart from the fanatical peace seeking journalists, none of the many suggestions en route about publicity on radio, television or newspapers had ever materialised. But the RSA office in Delhi take the view that my presence would do the company name no harm, with the result that two days after my arrival I am driven to a television studio to record an interview for 'Good Morning, India'. Naively expecting a degree of preparation, I have barely got my breath back from climbing the stairs, when I am on the sofa with two heavily made up presenters grinning at me. The PR lady had given me an RSA T-shirt, as well as a typed script singing corporate praises and instructions to mention the company name as frequently as possible. In amongst the inevitable questions about peace, this is beginning to feel like a very bad idea.

A précis of my background appears on the autocue which the woman reads at breathtaking speed and this is followed with questions from the man. Having barely made myself comfortable, it is over. My first appearance on television would last about two minutes and nobody has thought to ask me about the black eyes and bruises.

I then discover that there is a second part to this cameo – the practical. Returning the following day with the bike and empty panniers, I am asked to re-enact a normal day: attach the panniers in a car park, set off into heat haze of Delhi eventually to return to the car park, unclip the panniers and walk up the studio stairs! It is so insane and improbable, most especially when the trendy and ambitious cameraman hangs upside down out of the taxi (which I am paying for), keen to film from interesting angles and asking me to accommodate his needs by cycling slowly alongside. Oh well, at least I know the right man for fixing bikes should there be another crash. This all takes an hour and I feel a sense of imbalance here. People in Delhi see millions of bikes on the road every day so however arty this footage might be, surely there would be more interest in those fundamental questions of how I got here and where I intend to go next. I hadn't even been asked my age. (Sadly, the promise of the video of this programme never materialised. Perhaps not fifteen minutes of fame, but it would at least have been one for the grandchildren.)

Being the guest at an ex-pats party sets off a remarkable chain of events. The host heads up the Smith Kline Beecham operation, producing tons of Horlicks for local consumption. A hot comforting pre-bedtime drink, associated in my mind with dark, cold winter nights, this beggared belief in the Indian climate. He suggests that I visit the factory and then go on to Simla in the Himalayan foothills, a town which had been a major British centre during the days of the Empire. This was the place of my mother's birth – never in my most improbable wishes have I imagined that it would be possible for me to visit the town. It is an easy decision, so cycling is put to one side while I take to the trains and buses.

Chris arranges for me to stay in the SKB guest houses at each destination. My feeling of being looked after, not just by the elaborate hospitality of the makers of Horlicks, but by greater forces is reinforced yet again.

Amongst the more memorable conversations at the party was that with the ambassador from Argentina. When he learned about my accident he said 'Have you asked yourself why it happened? There is a very strong symbolism connected to this and you must think about the message behind it. You came to an abrupt and unscheduled stop. You should reflect on the meaning.'

(It is only weeks later that I could make a connection. Had the crash not happened I would have still been on the road at the time of the party. I would therefore never have met Chris and the opportunity to visit Simla could not have arisen. Surely too potent to be mere coincidence?)

From my privileged position as passenger in a car with a driver, I witness Indian roads from an entirely different aspect. Met off the train, the journey to the SKB factory premises is just less than an hour and during this time the driver has his foot to the floor and one hand on the hooter which he uses incessantly. The targets of this perpetual racket are the never ending stream of bicycles, scooters, motorbikes, cycle rickshaws, scooter rickshaws, tractors and carts drawn by just about everything from humans to any animal with a hoof and it serves no purpose other than to make me wish I had my earplugs with me as well as a blindfold. He has been instructed to take me sightseeing after being encouraged to 'take rest' which gives him another opportunity to break the land speed record. Such are the risks he takes in squeezing past every other moving or stationery object that he tucks in both wing mirrors as a safety measure. This leaves breathing in as the final option to narrow the already terrifyingly narrow gaps.

The drive a couple of days later is to catch the train to Simla and is much longer. This time two young men have been assigned to the task. They drive at walking pace, the horn redundant. As they speak no English it is necessary to keep my concerns to myself – there is a train to catch. With perfect precision we arrive with half an hour to spare. They assist me in buying a ticket, carry my luggage (how strange it is to be without my bicycle), point me in the direction of the ladies toilet, find the right platform, select a carriage and seat for me and then sit protectively nearby until the train departs. Throughout, their heads wobble from side to side, a unique Indian gesture that can be interpreted in so many ways and is impossible to mimic. The majority of passengers are backpackers who are mesmerised by the whole performance. My appearance does not merit this level of attention.

Stepping into the quaint train is like stepping into the past and it, like the Indian heads, wobbles each time a passenger gets on or off. Chugging slowly through the wonderful lower slopes of the mountains, the air cools with every chug. Station names are in the format of the London Underground and each station master is dressed in a starched Persil white uniform carrying a red and a green flag, each of which is waved enthusiastically at the appropriate moments.

The journey takes several hours through breathtaking scenery and the sight of Simla, perched precariously on a mountain side and highlighted in the evening sun, is a deeply emotional experience. The three days I spend there are peaceful, meditative and reflective.

I have decided that after cycling to Agra, home of the Taj Mahal, I will catch a train to Calcutta. My visa does not allow me time to cycle the entire breadth of the country and Simla has provided an unexpected Mecca. The heat is proving beyond insufferable (for a brief few days in the comparative cool of the mountain, the texture of my skin ceased to resemble that of chewed gum), the pollution revolting (surely the equivalent of smoking several hundred cigarettes a day) and my body is disappearing. It is impossible to judge, but I know I have lost a great deal of weight. And perhaps most relevant, there is no 'reward' for all the effort needed to cover the daily mileage – just straight mile after straight mile of slog. To cover the distance in the comfort of an air conditioned overnight sleeper has an irresistible appeal.

But there are still some miles of cycling left and the balance to my recent days of fat cat life is quickly restored on the first night back on the road. My search for accommodation results in being led by two young men on a scooter to a temple in Hodal. All previous attempts to sleep in temples have been thwarted for various reasons and I am very excited.

On arrival, what starts with the janitor as a sign language enquiry erupts into a full scale verbal brawl as dozens of onlookers become involved. I am bewildered at the level of emotion. It gradually becomes clear that beds do not become available until after seven o'clock in the evening. It is just gone noon and the argument is about whether or not to allow me to stay or send me off to wile away seven hours. Because of my pre-dawn start, the obligatory seventy miles have been covered and the only thing on my mind is rest, in its full and essential sense (as opposed to Indian version which is more about passing time). The charge for the room is fifty one rupees, so it seems reasonable to offer one hundred rupees to cover the extra use. He is furious and goes ballistic – I have clearly offended him deeply but cannot imagine why. The crowd manage to calm things down and a compromise is reached – I am allowed to stay in the courtyard. I hope I manage to convey my extreme and genuine gratitude.

Within minutes I have collapsed on my bed mat, covered from head to toe with the sarong (what an invaluable versatile item this is proving to be) and a South African baseball cap over my face – a psychedelic mummy! It's all a futile effort to keep the unrelenting flies at bay but their persistence outrivals mosquitoes, whose presence I have come to prefer. I am awoken from a sound sleep by giggling and when I poke my head out, there are thirty pairs of teenage eyes staring at me. These girls come to the temple from school each week for a sewing class but this is the chance to practise their English.

To the obligatory three questions, they add a fourth and entirely original one. 'What is the name of your husband?' I choose to lie and answer 'Fred'. I have discovered that the truth requires too much explanation and the limited knowledge of English often makes this impossible. Anyway, there probably isn't a word for *'divorced'* in the land of the arranged marriage.

I am finally invited to check in – a delightful contrast to the earlier animosity. Even the janitor and his family are smiling. I am directed to a room where an older man is sitting behind a table and in front of him is a large registration ledger – the sort of leather bound book one might associate with offices in the Forties. He spends ten minutes meticulously ruling vertical columns across the double page spread. The ruler is half the length of the page and he is concerned that the lines should be parallel and exactly join up; then each column is given a heading. Eventually he is ready to take down my details. My passport defeats him and sign language serves no purpose in this situation, with the result that only four of the twenty five columns reflect any information. My name, my age, where I come from and the name of my father! I hand over the fifty one rupees and he gives me back twenty rupees. I have become entitled to a massive discount and will never know why.

The night brings an intrusion more menacing than either flies or mosquitoes. Because of the inevitable power cut, the building is dark and worse by far the fan is not working. (As primitive as they may be, these fans do make a difference. Without them I feel as if I might dissolve. One can understand why the punka wallah gained such prestige in the days of the British Empire.) Returning from an irritating midnight trip to a disgusting loo, which is in a corner of the courtyard and not a place to visit in bare feet or linger too long, I see a man. He is standing near the entrance and approaches me to shake my hand. A strange encounter at such an hour, not least of all because I have my sarong wrapped around me leaving my shoulders bare. The handshake goes on much too long and I struggle to withdraw my hand from his crushing grip. Assuming him to be the night porter (normal practice throughout Asia in all hotels) this is nevertheless unusual behaviour. I head back to my room and he follows close behind. There is no misunderstanding my lack of pleasure at this encounter and when he grabs me, I shove him away. I manage to slam the door, but there is no lock – perhaps that explains the discount.

I am furious, rather than frightened and Alchemy proves the perfect bodyguard. My tactics for these early morning departures is to have all the panniers clipped on the racks, leaving only the minimal business of packing a few items before leaving. It not only saves times but if the electricity is off (as has so often been the case) it is pitch dark and there is danger of leaving things behind. Perched against the door, the weight of the bike will not prevent him entering but at least it will make a hell of a noise when it falls over. With luck he might trip over it and break his randy little neck. His continued banging wakes up the young man whom I had spent most of the evening talking to. He is on the floor above but by some strange architectural arrangement there is a connecting open grate in a communal wall.

'What is the matter, Pam? What's all the shouting and banging about? Have you got a problem?' I had never felt in real danger but his concerned voice is very comforting.

'There's a man who is trying to get into my room. He just keeps banging on the door and saying something. I thought he was on duty as the night porter but I must have got that wrong.'

'OK, don't worry, I'll be right down.'

This is the cue for the man to disappear and moments later my rescuer is in the room looking very worried. 'What did he look like' he asks.

'Very thin, medium height, straight black hair, dark skin, dressed in that white cotton two piece' I tell him (thinking *'that should narrow it down to several million'*).

'There's no point in calling the police now. They are the other side of the town and they wouldn't come anyway. He must have been passing – the temple gates are never locked. I'll go to my room now, but be sure and call me if he comes back.'

As coincidences go, that took the biscuit. Not the one about there being someone to help me – I have become used to that. But about this man being there at that moment I chose to go to the loo. Sleep is impossible, however. Not through worrying about his return, but the flies have spread the message. Their day shift is over and it is now the turn of the mosquitoes to come and check out what is on the menu.

Chapter Fifteen

The concept of not being able to tell Indian people apart is mirrored to me during my visit to the Taj Mahal. Anil, the brother of one of the girls in the RSA office, has offered to be my guide and while we sit in the shade watching the world pass us by, a large group of predominately male European tourists stand nearby, prompting Anil to observe 'I wouldn't recognise one from the other. They all look the same to me'.

Anil had visited the Taj Mahal many times and I welcomed his knowledge and enthusiasm. A very familiar sight from television and photographs, it is impossible to comprehend the enormity and beauty of the place unless one is there. We have spent most of the day wandering around or just sitting and absorbing the atmosphere.

He has a scooter which makes travelling around the town simple and with him by my side to ensure no misunderstandings, I buy the train ticket and reserve a seat. However, nervous after my experience in Sofia, I ask Anil to get confirmation that there will be absolutely no complications about having Alchemy on the train. What a silly question – this is India, the land of the bicycle.

'No problem madam' the ticket office assures me.

Our evening meal demonstrates again the contrasting values. We each have a selection of eight vegetarian dishes, an enormous feast, but I am sticking firmly to my rule of never drinking tap water, so order a small bottle at a cost of fifteen rupees – the same cost as my entire meal.

With plenty of time to spare, I have arrived at Tunla and begin to lose that feeling of security – what is it about that phrase *'no problem'* that has come to represent everything but? It is when the Station Master redirects me to the Parcel Office that loud ominous bells begin to ring.

A charming official speaking perfect English tells me 'Madam, I much regret that the bicycle cannot travel on the same train as you. This is because the luggage van is locked when the train leaves Delhi and it cannot be opened again until arrival in Calcutta. But this is no problem *(those words again)* because the bicycle can travel safely on the next train.'

'When is that' I ask, already knowing that I can never allow the bicycle and me to be separated.

'It is the Kalka Express and leaves here at six o'clock tonight.'

This is more than eight hours after my train but I sense a solution. 'Well, that's OK. I will spend the time here and then catch that train myself.'

'Many apologies, madam, but this is not possible. All the seats will be reserved. There will be no place for you and in any case the ticket you have is not transferable.'

'My entire life is represented in this bicycle. If it is stolen or lost, or even broken, my journey will have to end. It is a risk that I absolutely cannot take. Please, please – there must be a way it can be done.'

Short of bursting into tears or tendering him a bribe (the offer of my body would not have impressed him – my skin now resembles something that could be turned into handbags and *'weathered'* translates as looking twenty years older), I do everything possible to persuade him to change his mind.

'It is against the rules, madam' becomes his mantra. 'I cannot do this. The rules don't allow.'

I can't even accuse him of being an obnoxious Job's Worth. He is polite, co-operative and patient but nevertheless will not budge. This has much to do with his faith in the ability of the railways to ensure that The Team will be reunited. That's all very well, but....

He has telephoned home to tell his teenage sons about my presence and they arrive at the station curious to know about my journey. They are absolutely delightful and speak excellent if somewhat quaint English.

'That is a magnificent age and very much to your credit, ma'am' is their observation when hearing how old I am.

With an hour still to go before my train arrives, they carry everything except me to the correct platform, set me up in the comfort of a private office where the fan accompanies the start of my nervous breakdown.

Adding to my gibbering wreck status is the fact that as much as I have a ticket with a reserved seat, on purchasing this, the highly modern computerised system at the ticket office indicated that, in fact, I am really on stand-by – second in the queue. There had been a reassurance that this would be *'no problem'*.

'Don't be concerned' Anil translated the clerk's words. 'A seat will become available. You are sure to get on the train.' Sitting in this small office awaiting an unknown fate, the prospect of cycling the distance is beginning to feel a preferable alternative.

The train arrives on time but as it is two miles long I have first to find the coach referred to on my *'reservation'*. I have engaged a porter who is so old that he is not only incapable of running up and down the platform to find the coach, but I end up having to carry everything. The next ten minutes take on pantomime proportions. After finding my seat and having a major row with the porter who believes he has been under tipped (I had taken the precaution of asking my friend in the Parcels Office what would be appropriate and doubled his recommendation), the steward for my part of the train says that it will be quite in order to have the bicycle alongside me in the corridor. Feeling weak from delight, I sprint to the far end of the platform to find that the charming man from the Parcels Office has managed to unlock the luggage van only to find that there is no space. Not even the pump for the tyres would have fitted, never mind the whole bicycle.

'It's not a problem – really no problem' I shriek and proceed to tell him that I have been given permission to have Alchemy in the carriage with me.

His reaction – back to the mantra 'It's against the rules, madam. I cannot let you take the bicycle in the passenger part of the train. The railway company does not allow it.'

'But the steward says it's OK. Isn't that all that matters? For crying out aloud, please, just let me take the bike.'

There follows a bizarre tug of war as I try to steal my own bicycle. But, of course, time is ticking by and as much of a nightmare as this is, worse by far would be to see the train pulling out with all my luggage on board. There is no choice but to race back down the platform, but by now I have forgotten which carriage I am in. The steward is standing at the open door looking out for me and he grabs me as the train begins to move. I collapse, breathless and distraught saying over and over again 'What have I done? What have I done?'

Any idea of not getting a seat is farcical as I have the whole compartment (supposedly meant to accommodate six people) to myself. It is air conditioned and the entire journey to Calcutta is spent horizontal and comatose.

The railways are a legacy from the British and I am to benefit from this on arrival in Calcutta as there is a spacious Ladies Room with every facility imaginable, including showers. Knowing my panniers will be safe, I set about establishing how The Rules stipulate that I retrieve my *'parcel'*. I am redirected again and again to several different offices in a vast station and seem to have confounded everyone as answers vary from 'You will have to wait two days for us to process everything in the luggage van. This always takes much time.' Or 'Wait at your hotel and we will contact you.' Or 'Collect it from the Parcels Office two hours after the train has arrived.' Or 'It is best you meet the train and take it off yourself.'

Of course it is the last option that I choose. When the time does come, just in case there might be a single corpuscle of my body that has not already been overrun by panic, another major drama is played out with more rushing from several information offices to arrivals board to station master (and at one point even trying to understand the announcements over the loudspeaker system – I've never managed that at Paddington) to establish exactly which platform the Kalka Express would arrive at. To my delight the luggage wagon is right behind the engine but is empty when opened. There is a real danger that my heart will stop beating until one of the uniformed men informs me 'There is another one at the end of the train.' If it is possible to run a four minute mile holding your breath, that is what I do, only to find this one firmly locked. Standing on the platform are the two guards who have travelled with the train, two officials from the Parcels Office and six Railway Police carrying rifles. We are all waiting for the key. Nobody is equipped with either two way radio or mobile phone so we wait and wait.

'What is it that you want?' one of the officials asks me.

'My bicycle should have been loaded on this train at Tunla. I have the receipt for it here' I reply, showing one of the several forms which had been completed.

'Do you mean a red one?' asks one of the guards. It's as well I'm not the feinting sort. I feel so overwhelmed with relief that I am speechless and hugging Indian men is not an option.

We all stand there for over an hour during which time one of the men from the Parcels Office is dispatched to find either the key or someone who would know where it is. I have become brilliant at imagining nightmare scenarios and the next thing that comes to mind is – what if the train leaves on its return journey with the bike still in the luggage van? With this vision being played out in three dimensional Technicolor in my mind's eye, I begin to make a huge fuss verging on tantrums, with the result that three of the men begin to heave on the door and it flies open. It had never been locked – it was just jammed. Unbelievably Alchemy is the sole occupant. My ecstatic and unrestrained relief at our reunion is something that I doubt those men will ever forget.

Chapter Sixteen

It is time to leave India.

As it is impossible to cross the land borders into Burma I have to fly to Bangkok and after Alchemy's previous bruising experience I am extremely nervous at the prospect. The drama this time is at the beginning of the flight rather than on arrival.

'Are you carrying any batteries or knives?' the uniformed woman at the entrance to the departure lounge asks me.

'Yes, I have several batteries and a Swiss army knife.'

'Then I must ask you to unpack your luggage. We have to remove these during the flight because they represent a source of danger.'

All these items are invaluable to me and as I am not at all convinced that I will ever see them again, I protest vigorously. 'They cannot possibly be dangerous. They are packed so tightly it would take the whole flight to find them. Please, just leave everything alone.'

But, once again the rule book is thrown up in my face and the entire contents of two panniers are spread about the counter. 'What's this?' she repeats several times as she rummages through items such as water purifier, short-wave radio, medicines, tool kit, rape alarm. Finally, having satisfied her curiosity, she removes several batteries and the invaluable knife. Not a day has passed when it hasn't been needed. By doing so she probably saved her life as the purpose for today could well have been to slit her throat.

'Can I help?' she asks as I attempt to recreate the conjuring trick of repacking everything.

Arriving in Bangkok just before midnight, the safest way into the city centre is on the airport bus where I get talking to travellers from Belgium, Australia and America. This chance meeting enhances my time in the city as we all book into a hotel together and spend time looking around.

The tourist area of town, Khao San Road, is a backpackers' paradise. It is at its liveliest in the early hours of the morning and the food stalls sell such delicacies as cockroaches and beetles. Could this perhaps be a form of pest control? What a scam – convincing tourists to eat insects that back home would be to crushed underfoot and prompt a visit from the local health and hygiene inspectors.

I am very aware that my stamina is below par. I feel wobbly and lethargic and it is obvious that I have lost a great deal of weight. The solution lies in a million calories, but consuming them has once again become an ordeal; my stomach is in reject mode. In India it was not just hot air temperatures that were so debilitating, but also the hot spicy food for which I seemed to have a very low tolerance. I loved the tea laced with cardamom (although pint mugs would have been more appreciated than the tiny glasses in which it is always served) and the fruit salads sprinkled with an allspice seasoning, but the tongue burning, palate stripping main course dishes had defeated me.

One evening I spotted a stall with a man frying potatoes in a large stainless steel pan. It was a chance to get a take away of untainted potatoes to gorge on so I seized the opportunity and ordered a portion. Having cooked them, he was about to squirt a curry sauce on to the potatoes before serving them to me, but my shriek of panic stopped him in time. My salivating anticipation was short lived. Even the minimal residue in the pan from previous use was enough to contaminate my meal to the point that I could barely eat it – the potatoes had taken on a vindaloo quality.

The appalling consequence is that the much anticipated food of Thailand, a vegetarian's paradise with a real choice of non-spicy vegetables, is proving to be a struggle to eat and so there is little sign of that exhausted feeling disappearing. As always there are compensations. One is a significant drop in temperature which in itself makes cycling so much easier. And the other is that Thailand does not have a third world feel to it. Not only is the air clean – pollution is no longer visible in black clouds of exhaust fumes – but it is also silent, because drivers have both hands on the steering wheel rather than one glued to the horn.

The difference between India and Thailand could be symbolically summed up at the scene of a broken down bus. This had been a frequent sight in India where the passengers would squat, silent and resigned on the side of the road. In Thailand, however, I only witnessed one such incident and here the passengers were pacing around agitatedly, all talking on their mobile phones.

The disappointment is the change in culture. Whereas in Pakistan and India everybody felt entitled to talk to me, in Thailand this is not proving to be the case. I am eating all meals by myself and this makes such a significant difference. Even if restricted to sign language, use of maps and calculators, these chance encounters are the essence of my day's experience.

There is one memorable exception. Because it is raining hard I have taken the opportunity to shelter in a petrol station and decide to have something to eat. A young man who had filled his car up comes over out of curiosity. When I show him my route on the map and he realises that I intend to cycle through Laos, he is so visibly shaken that he has to sit down. He then proceeds to indicate how dangerous this would be and that it is imperative I change my mind.

My more urgent need is to find a hotel for the night and I ask him to write the name down so that I can show this on arrival at the town, some five miles further on. I think I have said goodbye to him, but instead he is sitting in his car just outside the petrol station waiting for me and gestures that he intends to lead me to the door of the hotel. This means driving at well below boy racer speed for a considerable time, but it is his choice and once we arrive in bizarre convoy, he checks inside the hotel, helps me in with my luggage and with a huge smile on his young face, drives off with a wave. There is such a thing as a *'free lunch'* – whatever form it comes in.

My journey through Thailand is plagued not just with mosquitoes, persistent companions since Bulgaria, but unceasing horror stories about Laos. More colourful and insistent than the well worn bad neighbour syndrome, whenever I show my map to indicate where from and where to, a look of terror appears on their faces which I am finding disconcerting. One woman mimed a scenario of my panniers being snatched at the point of a gun. Everyone is genuinely concerned. It is not out of the question to backtrack to Malaysia and proceed south to Singapore but I'm too exhausted to contemplate it.

It is in Thailand that the CatEye computer dies. My relationship with the information supplied by this computer can best be described as addictive, obsessive and compulsive. About the size of a sports wrist watch, it has provided comprehensive details about the day's ride; not just daily and overall totals of mileage and the related cycling time, but average speed and top speed, current air temperature and accumulated altitude gained. Part of the excitement at the end of each day is to record the statistics which would have their own story to tell on my return.

But my obsession with it is not concerned with the long term, it is all to do with the here and now. Every hour throughout the day I would check through each aspect of information which would give the background to my progress. This is something that can be done on the move and it has become an indirect form of encouragement. It is also a welcome distraction to the endless pedalling. Except perhaps in India, where it was the worst and best of friends. Having cycled say fifty or sixty miles, the combination of heat and exhaustion would make the remaining ten very tough. The temptation had been to check the computer every five minutes in the absurd hope that the distance would miraculously have evaporated along with my energy and sweat.

The death of the CatEye is not the end of my effort to record the journey and feed my habit. I purchase another at Nong Khai for £2.50. It survives long enough to cross the border into Laos, three miles down the road, before it too stops. (I buy a spare tyre at the same shop which I hope will last somewhat longer.) It turns out that its failure is not terminal, rather more a coma from which it would emerge occasionally. This burst of life could not be linked with any identifiable reason such as rain, grit, mud or a bad connection but makes any idea of recording hourly, daily or overall progress fall into the realms of guesswork. Proving that third time is not necessarily lucky, computer number three would be purchased in Hong Kong. Another CatEye, it performs perfectly until the temperatures drop below 6°C when it goes into hibernation and only direct sunshine will coax it back to life. By this time, I have to accept the symbolic message that to represent the achievement of the journey in statistics would not be important.

When I arrive in Nong Khai I am fortunate, once again through a process of stopping and asking, to discover a guest house – real backpackers' territory – and as it is only the second such experience so far I find it a welcome novelty. It sits on the banks of the Mekong River and at £1.85 per night, is the perfect place to recuperate for a few days. The Mat Mee is run by an English man, Julian and his younger Thai wife (not an unusual combination in this part of the world, but I have yet to see the reverse arrangement) and some very traditional English food is on the menu. Porridge, muesli, yoghurt, salad, boiled eggs, cheese sandwiches – nectar to my abused stomach. The days pass in very undemanding ways exchanging stories with many others.

Lewie, a wandering Kiwi about my age and seeking pastures new. Ulrich and Katherin, a newly married German couple on an extended honeymoon. Bob, a veteran hippy, the living version of a rolling stone (certainly hadn't gathered any moss, just long white hair and beard) who meditated, smoked dope and ran his organic farm with the help of WOOFAS. Mike, a discontent overweight older man who walks with the aid of two sticks and does nothing but complain. 'I've been travelling for three months. I think it's time I went home' he observes. I did have to wonder why he had ever left. I go on a day's sightseeing with two couples. Our transport is a small pick-up in the back of which are five unsecured dining chairs in order that we may have an improved view.

The decision is made to treat myself to a new trio of knickers. I have shrunk to the point that the current batch are in danger of descending around my knees and anyway no washing powder could ever restore them to their former whiter than white glory. The irony is that in Thailand, where my height of five feet eight inches gives me giant status, it is only the extra large size that will fit.

Chapter Seventeen

After a few days the porridge has revitalised the parts that Indian food failed to reach and it is time to move on so I cycle the few miles to Friendship Bridge. There is a moment of deep disappointment on discovering that it is impossible to cycle across. I am mortified, not just because there is an indescribable excitement cycling over enormous bridges, but this one is such a landmark. About a mile across the Mekong river, it carries traffic in both directions but cycling is forbidden. A bureaucratic nonsense but in spite of my best efforts there is no negotiation.

The only alternative is on a bus, already overcrowded with locals. What I am completely unprepared for is the immediately detectable change of atmosphere on disembarking at the Laos end. Porters and tuc-tuc drivers are always on the look out for the foreigner ('*the sucker*') and so they all swarm towards me as I hand down the four panniers. When Alchemy follows they realise that this means no business for any of them and they all burst out laughing while they hold the bicycle and help me load up. This is in marked contrast to the reaction in the previous three countries which had inevitably been one of open disappointment, even overt hostility. These positive omens are confirmed during the short ride to Vientiane during which literally everyone, including rickshaws and cyclists, acknowledges me by hooting, smiling, waving, saying hello.

The question is often asked 'Why are you cycling alone?' The simple answer is that one is not spoiled for choice when it comes to looking for someone to cycle around the world with. And even if there were several, just how many miles would the two travel before conflicts arose? For me the thought of a companion had never arisen. The preconceptions were that being alone one would make one more vulnerable but I viewed this as an asset. Strangers would be more predisposed to approaching a person who was by themselves. Whenever I had travelled with groups, whether large or small, we had been cocooned from the local population. Any discussion was contained within the group. To some extent I believe that this also applies to couples, who have the travel book clutched between them and discuss options of food, hotels, routes between themselves. The way it has mostly worked for me is all I have had to do is stop and within minutes at least one person would approach me. It also has allowed me to be guided by gut feeling and intuition and given me great freedom to make spontaneous decisions. (Remember my 'kidnapping' in Pakistan by the wooden-legged shopkeeper and all those warnings about danger and fanatic fundamentalists? Just one of the many highlights of my journey which perhaps perceived wisdom and a cycling companion might have censored.) It didn't feel selfish – it has been more a matter of capitalising on my single and vulnerable status.

But things are about to change. While withdrawing US dollars from a bank in Thailand a Frenchman and his girlfriend, also there to sort out money matters, had noticed my well used Asia Overland book. They approached me and with synchronicity working overtime it was decided that he and I would join forces in Vientiane and continue our journey north into China together. He had cycled from France and his girlfriend, over for a month's holiday, was about to return home. He was the instigator as he hadn't cycled a single mile on his own and was very keen for me to become his travelling companion – purely in the cycling sense. With all the warnings about Laos, it seemed that fate had dealt me yet another trump. Vietnam headed my list of most eagerly anticipated countries, but China held more than a degree of apprehension. I had heard too many stories from backpackers who had experienced difficulties. On balance it seemed like a good idea but I did have one major concern. Jean-Yves was young and male which would inevitably mean that his cycling agenda would be turbo charged. He had assured me that he took a very relaxed attitude about how far and how fast and would be more than happy for me to dictate both. We would have to see.

Our rendezvous is half past ten at the Scandinavian Bakers – another great advantage of a travel book and emails – and part of me is secretly hoping that he would have headed off. But no, he has decided to wait and over my first cup of coffee in months accompanied by a jam doughnut, we discuss plans. Needing a Vietnamese visa, he has discovered that the quick and painless way is to hand the whole scary business over to a travel agent. The visa will cost no more than if one went to the Embassy in person ($55), but the agent does all the leg work and hanging around. There is a moment of panic when the passport and accompanying documents are returned to me. On the application form, which the travel agent had completed, they have chosen my profession as *'schoolteacher'* and forged my signature! Would the immigration at the Vietnam border notice this and if so, what then?

It is in Vientiane that I experience real rain – as in monsoon – which makes the prospect of cycling very different because within minutes the roads have become red rivers. Short of having Wellington boots and umbrella, I have been fully prepared since Pakistan but suddenly *'waterproof'* takes on a whole new meaning. My luggage has a Bohemian look. As none of the panniers are waterproof (at the time of purchase their sole function had been a weekend in the Isle of Wight) four sturdy heavy gauge polythene bags have been adapted to do the job. To all intents and purposes each pannier has its own prototype drysuit at a cost of nothing and the result is spectacularly successful.

Where mangoes were the eating highlight of my day in Pakistan and India, in Laos it is pineapples. Imagine my delight when buying one from a stall to have it prepared there on the spot so that it would be ready to eat – a take-away pineapple. With precision, skill and a very sharp knife, the girl sets about skinning the fruit with deft incisions, wasting none of the flesh but miraculously removing those hundreds of sharp, teeth invading black bits. It is a remarkable performance, a street cabaret, and within five minutes I walk away with a giant and juicy pineapple lollipop.

Looking at Laos on my small scale map it is only an inch wide but within this inch are some serious mountains. There is a major decision to be made: to cycle directly over them to Vietnam on flooded muddy potholed roads, or to cycle five hundred miles further by travelling south on a more major road. Jean-Yves is keen to go the shorter route but my concern is that my fitness level will have plummeted, indeed vanished somewhere in the plains of India and therefore the longer route seems a wiser choice. So, we do it the French way – and this is the dawning of truth. The loss of my control. Still concerned about rumours of danger in Laos, and certainly apprehensive about China, I choose to go with him. His intention is to cycle all the way to Beijing, so if it works we would stay together until I peel off right to Hong Kong, still another 1,500 miles, with a great deal of pedalling and puffing in between and plenty of time to re-think.

We set off as feared in monsoon conditions. It seems that there is more danger of drowning than being shot or dying of starvation. Miraculously, within an hour the rain has disappeared along with all traffic and red mud, and we have the roads to ourselves. There isn't even a pothole to remind us we are cycling in an impoverished country and the occasional bus or car which drives past makes a point of waving a friendly greeting. Progress is wonderful and the day is complete when two elephants approach. They cannot qualify in the wild life trail as these elephants are working – each carrying a heavy load and guided by a man. A timeless moment.

We develop a great breakfast routine. Part of the country's French heritage ensures that warm baguettes (the perfect vehicle for bananas) are on sale everywhere. So, after an hour or so of cycling we find somewhere quiet and comfortable and build a huge banana butty each – excellent cycling fodder. The landscape is so different from anything so far. The whole country appears to be one enormous paddy field. The villages are frequent but very primitive and absolutely everyone turns out to shout and wave with big grins, particularly on the faces of the children who are delighted to have even this short distraction. Of course we wave back with our best imitation of 'savardee' (or so it sounds) which we take for 'hello'. All those rumours spread by the Thais about needing a bullet proof vest are proving exceedingly exaggerated – perhaps there's no need for a travelling companion after all.

The destination each day is dictated by a town big enough to have a guest house. Although we both have tiny tents, we have yet to spot a square metre of land to pitch them on. An inflatable dinghy would have been more suitable.

The cost of accommodation is per room, rather than per person (much of Jean-Yves' motivation for wanting me around) but what neither of us have bargained on is that hotels and guest houses allocate the minimal amount of space to each room – barely enough to contain a double bed. Jean-Yves is having a real problem with this and so on the first evening we waste a good hour checking out other hotels, only to find they are all the same – tiny room filled with tiny double bed. Thus, each night in Laos would find him stuck to the wall as chewing gum to the pavement, while I play my part by doing my best not to fall out onto the floor the other side. Either way the entente does remain very, but not too, cordiale and exhaustion, yes even for him, ensures that sleeping is not a problem.

The evening meals are challenging. My temporarily adopted non-vegetarian regime is less upsetting here as the very idea of factory or intensive farming has to be out of the question in these surroundings. Instead, the problem must be catching the chicken, duck, goose, turkey, cow and even

Vietnamese pot bellied pig – their natural habitat is roaming free on the roads and surroundings. The popular dish at the street stalls (café would be an exaggeration) is a wishy washy chicken soup. The *'chicken'* is those bits that would normally be thrown into the stockpot or the bin, and the whimpish noodles are packed with barely sufficient calories to cover ten miles next day. Occasionally there is rice on offer (not unreasonable as we are surrounded by the crop) with somewhat more identifiable parts of the chicken – enough to cycle fractionally further.

Next day we check into a primitive guest house. It is on stilts as are most of the village homes, with walls made of woven banana leaves, not best known for their sound insulation quality. It is Friday – karaoke night – and the bar appears to be the hang out for local drunks. (The time is just three o'clock and one is already snoring on the floor.) The karaoke machine is fired up to eardrum bursting decibels and made more intolerable when someone with a voice worse than mine (little comfort drawn from that) grabs the microphone and starts singing. The owner proudly informs us that this would continue until two o'clock tomorrow morning.

We take flight, only to check in to what turns out to be the local knocking shop. The clue is in the heart shaped hotel sign and the pink, very pink outside walls. But Friday night is karaoke night, even here. With the advantage of brick walls, this seems the lesser of two evils but the invitation to join the gathering revellers is easy to turn down. The source of electricity is a generator so if it all gets too much we could sabotage their worst efforts by shutting it down. That will just leave the constant background noise of the cicadas.

In the morning we watch a serene sunrise evolve behind the mountains which are shrouded in an atmospheric mist. I know it is an illusion, because it is these imposing mountains that we are about to tackle and all essence of calm and tranquillity will evaporate as I pedal and puff my way ever upwards. My dread is not that they will prove impossible but that it will take me so much longer than a young and fit Frenchman. And I am not wrong. To the pedalling and puffing should be added pushing and exhaustion – the sort where every muscle and brain cell is screaming *'give up and lie down'*. When a local bus stops to offer me a lift, it is a mixture of pride, bloody mindedness and will power that prevents me from accepting, as well as the fact that this would have denied me the reward of the inevitable descent – which brings unimaginable joy and rushing rivers of adrenaline.

The second day in the mountains has a sting in the tail. Our destination indicated on the map has not a single guest house, with or without Karaoke, drunks or pink hearts. Had I been travelling alone, the outcome would have been different as there is no doubt that accommodation could have been found with the villagers, but Jean-Yves is reluctant, indeed adamant that this is not an option and a further twenty five miles has to be cycled. (The local cycling club in Sussex consider thirty miles a decent Sunday ride – with stops for coffee, lunch and tea and carrying no more than a spare inner tube.) The road surface by now has deteriorated and the Brooks saddle and my bum are completely irreconcilable. Even the effort of smiling and replying to the cheery greetings is beyond me. It must seem so rude, but every ounce of energy and concentration is needed to keep going.

Chapter Eighteen

When we reach the Vietnam border my forged signature and invented career arouse no suspicion and the entry fee is $1. (The cost to enter Laos was been 20p.) But what is this 'entry fee'? We have already paid for the visas. Perhaps it funds the Christmas party or summer outing. The fact that there is nobody on duty when we arrive sets the somewhat casual scene and after waiting several minutes we have to go in search of a uniformed official. We are the only travellers, but this does not mean that the border is quiet.

There is an entirely different scenario being played out – a unique one way activity from Laos to Vietnam. Dozens of trucks are lined up on the Laos side unloading every imaginable type of electrical goods, as well as hundreds of cases of Red Bull and a variety of alcohol. The porters carrying these on their backs represent an ant-like activity and cross the border into Vietnam unchallenged. On the other side there are squadrons of men on motorbikes – well only just motorbikes, as these do not fall into the 1000cc BMW category. They resemble more a grown up scooter. Up to eighteen televisions would be loaded on to the back of a single bike which would then set off down the mountain. The sheer ingenuity of strapping the boxes on is utterly staggering. But, as we are to discover, there is nothing that the Vietnamese cannot carry on two wheels. In the coming days we spot an adult pig squished into a tailor made metal cocoon allowing no room for it to struggle; several piglets in similar cages; snakes; chickens; ducks. They are equally capable of fitting entire families on these scooters, two or three adults and five children. Crash helmets? Absolutely not.

The all too short twenty miles downhill produces an equivalent rise in temperature, but with less humidity at least there is no danger of my leaving a trail of sweat to bring the motorbikes skidding off the road. (Looking back, more water must have been consumed by me in these few months than in my entire life.) By the time we arrive at our planned stop we are both exhausted but worse by far is that we have already learned to hate the Vietnamese and we've only been in the country half a day.

During the long hard slog across the plain we were pestered for over an hour by two men on bicycles. They indicated that they wanted cigarettes and money, and anything or everything that we were carrying or wearing, including watches. They were very taunting and very aggressive, trying to grab at the bicycles or our gear. They would either cycle alongside or drop back talking loudly to each other. When they went quiet it was difficult not to keep glancing behind, but their presence was always indicated by the clanking of their very uncared for bicycles. Gone were the friendly Laos smiles and hellos. Instead everyone, including the women and children, yelled in a threatening and menacing way. They even succeeded in making *'hello'* sound offensive and sinister; *'Oy Oy'* is the phrase used to gain attention with a *'don't you dare ignore me'* tone to it.

We make it to Ben Thuy, the first sizeable town and find the only hotel. Things begin to look up when we manage to negotiate a significant fifty percent discount for the room which is huge, with two very large single beds miles apart and evidence that tea would be available in there as well. The appropriate forms are filled in, our passports checked and the money paid. But, when they give us the key they keep the passports, indicating that they are to be locked in a drawer overnight.

We are surrounded by a dozen young men and women, with no clear sign of which is the hotel manager. They have become extremely over excited at our presence and there is a hyper level of touching and giggling. They also make futile efforts to ride both the bicycles (not so much because of the weight but because their legs are about twelve inches too short). We are extremely eager to disappear to our room and start the recovery process but we are both adamant that our passports should be returned first. There is no justification or legal requirement to hold them and as we intend to leave at six o'clock, there is no guarantee that anyone will be around to return them. All this has to be communicated in a bizarre charade, to which their mimed response is the equivalent of *'over all our dead bodies'*.

One girl is holding both passports so I reach out to take them back. This results in a tug of war which I have no intention of losing and for good measure I also grab the cash that we paid for the rooms. All we have to do now is leave and suddenly pandemonium erupts. As we return to the bicycles the huge iron gates to the courtyard are locked with several chains and padlocks thus barring our only exit. Within minutes there is an impressive crowd on both sides of the gates. Is this *'stale mate'* or *'check mate'* or just *'no hope mate'*? There is a great deal of yelling, pointing and very accusing glares. Surely, no matter how desperate the hotel is for business, it could not be legal to deny potential customers the right to leave? Jean-Yves and I look helplessly and silently at each other. Escape is impossible, as is negotiation – even in this large crowd nobody speaks English (or perhaps just won't admit it – why intervene and end the cabaret?) Would we still be standing here come nightfall, dawn…. I feel confused and angry rather than frightened.

An hour passes and then a policeman on a motorbike arrives, much to my relief. He sits at a table opposite us and the crowd closes in. Definitely the best show in town. He demands our passports and it is impossible to refuse. (As part of a side show, they are passed amongst the throng who jeer at the photographs – not a very adult, official or encouraging performance.) All attention is focused on me and he indicates that I should give him money. There is much evidence in travel books about Vietnamese policemen demanding bribes, even from local residents never mind helpless tourists, so adamant refusal has to be the only answer. So we have a stand-off. More glaring and demanding on his part, more head shaking and stubbornness on mine. Next step – jail? And then what – call the British consulate? Perhaps carrying a mobile phone might have been a good idea. Another hour passes and it is Jean-Yves who identifies the cause.

He says quietly 'Pam, check the amount of money which you snatched back from the girl.'

'Why, what's that got to do with anything?' I say, looking puzzled.

'Just do it – check exactly how much money you have taken.'

Amidst all the drama, the fistful of *'dong'* that I had seized from her hand is still crumpled up at the top of a pocket in my bumbag. It hasn't been restored to its rightful place with the rest of my Vietnamese money. When I count the notes the amount is greater than we paid for the room! This is what all the commotion has been about. Assuming that the money she had in her hand was the money that had just been given to her, I had seized the lot. The excess amounted to less than one dollar. The power of communication, or in this case complete lack of it. A couple of very dodgy hours due to a complete misunderstanding.

How now to apologise on an international scale with sign language? This will turn out unequivocally to be my most high profile bad moment. Jean-Yves and I are both convinced that jail would be have been the inevitable next stage. However, having returned the money, there is a great deal of smirking at my efforts to say sorry and the padlocks and chains are removed. Almost an anti climax. In spite of the eighty miles already covered, adrenaline fuels the energy needed to cycle another twenty to the next town. My red face is not due this time to over exertion and takes a long time to fade.

The ride to Hanoi over the next two days can only be described as pure hell. Since setting off with Jean-Yves each day had been hard and *'arrival'* has become synonymous with *'totally knackered'*. Up until now it has seemed unimportant to divulge daily cycling statistics. But, because they are exceptional, here are a few facts for the six days leading to Hanoi. The average mileage per day was eighty nine and on three of these days we did between one hundred and five to one hundred and fifteen, necessitating one eight hour stint in the saddle and seven and a half hours on two other days. The average speed was fourteen and a half miles per hour. Just to emphasise how much this was stretching me, my average mileage up till then had been sixty seven miles per day, and the average speed varied between eleven to thirteen miles per hour. It was surprising that my heart, never mind my legs had not thrown in the towel. I felt entitled to be knackered. Every morning we were up and on the road by six o'clock.

Approaching Hanoi we are cycling along the road which travels north/south between Saigon and Hanoi. It is single carriageway and packed solid with traffic comprising mostly buses, then lorries and some cars and it is back to the hooting – constant, loud and obnoxious – and choking exhaust fumes. India and Pakistan paled in comparison with these guys because of the concentration of traffic. As if this isn't bad enough, passengers lean out of passing buses attempting to hit us and often succeeding. On at least three occasions the driver of a tractor or motor bike approaching from the opposite direction swerved across the road aiming straight at us and then laughing hysterically as he veered away at the last minute. Objects have been hurled from fields and if the tone of voice is anything to go by, so is abuse. The aggressive *'hellos'* and *'oy's'* are small fry compared to this nightmare. And on four further occasions we are shadowed and hassled by two male cyclists – not for five minutes but anything up to an hour. Absolutely no fun.

There isn't even a choice of getting on one of these buses as rumour has it that travelling by bus could seriously damage your luggage. Stories about keeping an eye on one backpack were intimidating enough, never mind a bicycle and four panniers. We make best headway by my tucking in behind the back wheel of Jean-Yves – slipstreaming – and it is astonishing just how much this really cuts down on the effort needed by the one behind. As long as Alchemy's front wheel does not stray more than a few inches from his back wheel, it is possible to keep up with his crippling speed. It is a revelation but it also demands full concentration as there is no margin for error. And there is the final danger that my only memory of the scenery through Vietnam will be the Frenchman's salty bum.

The French version of Lonely Planet makes it possible for Jean-Yves to do some impressive navigation to the door of a guest house in the centre of Hanoi. The only available accommodation is a minuscule three bed room (as in one bed and one bunk) and nowhere inside the building to accommodate the bikes, which would have to remain out on the pavement. Jean-Yves quite rightly insists that this is out of the question but my aching bum, lungs and legs are so utterly done in that I would happily negotiate for Alchemy to have my bed while I sleep on the pavement.

A tout picks up on our dilemma and quotes us $3 per night – considerably less than we were expecting to pay in the capital. We are sure there is a catch but there is only one way to find out which is to follow him. Trying to keep up with Jean-Yves on the open road has been difficult enough but trying to follow him following a motorbike through the crowded streets of Hanoi is the very last thing I need. Nothing can prepare you for the volume of everything: pedestrians, bicycles, scooters, motorbikes, cars and buses; the traffic equivalent of sardines, but all on the move. If I lose sight of that French bum now there is no fall back plan.

There is no catch apart from the fact that our room is on the third floor. It is less than a week since the hotel opened and nothing is too much trouble. All my luggage is carried up for me which is just as well as my legs can barely manage to get my scrawny body up the six flights. Most unexpected and most welcome is ... a bath, with an endless supply of really hot water. (My last bath was in Vienna.) My joy at getting into the steaming deep water is temporarily marred because when I lie down my lower spine and pelvic bone clatter and graunch against the bottom of the bath – more proof of missing flesh. I collapse into bed too tired to eat or sleep.

The Chinese Embassy is the only reason to stay in Hanoi and the application for a visa turns out to be very straightforward. It costs $30 with a four day collection time. Moving around the city as a single tourist proves an utter nightmare. Touts hassle constantly trying to sell everything from postcards to hammocks. (Just who on earth is going to spontaneously buy a hammock?) Whenever I buy food the street traders try and charge ten times the local rate. When I refuse they become genuinely angry. If I adopt an attitude of laughing and walking away the price drops dramatically. There is an attitude of resentment and any curiosity is very hostile. Because I find it intrusive and difficult to handle, I use the time to catch up on emails – internet cafés by the dozen packed with locals as well as tourists and unbelievably cheap – and trying to encourage food into my still reluctant system. I am beginning to believe that my eyes literally are bigger than my stomach. The television provides an unexpected diversion. Its constant flow of western films and American serials are dubbed into the Vietnamese language with every part being spoken in the dull monotones of a single female voice.

The lasting memories are of the street traders. Exclusively women who carry a pole across their shoulders from which swings a basket at either end and there is nothing that is not on offer – a mobile supermarket. Live ducks, chickens and fish, the same again but dead, hunks of unrecognisable meat, bread and cakes, doughnuts even, fruit, salad and vegetables (mostly unrecognisable) and luxuries such as flowers and plants. The loads would cripple a Surrey housewife, but these women have developed a lolloping gait and seem to be out there all day and day after day. There is no need to go shopping as everything in the world that you could possibly want is carried right past your door.

The men perform a similar exercise, but on bicycles loaded with the equivalent of perhaps the entire Tupperware selection, hundreds of baskets or larger livestock such as pigs. Most men wear a somewhat military style round green hat, similar to the old army tin hats, with a small brim and the chin strap pulled up over the top. They are also one of the many items that tourists are pestered to purchase when walking the city. I did suggest to Jean-Yves that we buy one, ceremoniously place it on the pavement and then stamp all over it. It has come to symbolise everything we loath about the country, but one confrontation with a policeman is perhaps enough.

The whole nation are much shorter than people in the West. Tables and chairs are often the size of those found in nursery schools back home. (This is also true in China.) Women compensate with platform shoes of oil rig dimensions. To see a woman not wearing them is exceptional. There is a rumour that A & E departments in Asian hospitals are full of broken ankles as a result and from all the evidence, it must be true. They even manage to cycle in them, wearing long white gloves and a straw hat (to keep the sun off their skin) and elaborate cotton face masks (a futile attempt to keep the pollution out of their lungs). Another amazing and not uncommon sight is a man cycling with a huge battery operated radio strapped to his handlebars and blaring out at full volume. Could this be propaganda for the passers-by or his own version of a personal stereo?

The rumour that Asian countries eat dog is true in Vietnam. The subject came up in a discussion about restaurants. Dog is considered a luxury food and it is possible to spot the expensive restaurants (those which serve dog) by the fact that there are motorbikes parked outside, rather than just bicycles.

The moment of truth – the thirty day visa for China is granted without a hiccup or a forged signature. It helps having perfected the art of using elbows or whatever else it takes to maintain one's place, or perhaps even improve on it, in a crowded room with no queuing system. The meek might well inherit the earth but they stand no chance of getting to the front of what is a scrum in the embassies of Asia. Woman and children first – forget it. It is also a great advantage being several feet taller than the Vietnamese.

Chapter Nineteen

Jean-Yves and I part company amicably on the outskirts of Hanoi. He is headed for Beijing and I am off to Hong Kong. Whatever my apprehensions of tackling the perceived difficulties and intimidations of China, I will be doing so on my own. If Vietnam, the country that I had so been looking forward to, proved so diabolical and daunting, just how bad would China be? I am about to find out. Apart from significant problems about foreigners being arrested for staying in the wrong hotel, there are more fundamental difficulties to be overcome. Numbers indicated by a hand using fingers might not be translated as such. What other interpretation could there possibly be to one or two fingers stuck up in the air! But, as I am to discover, the abacus is still used so what hope sign language. Whatever dramas or problems lie ahead, at least my legs are thrilled at the prospect of parting company with that French backside – the effort of keeping up with it had lived up to all my anxieties.

(The other major bonus would be no more intense curiosity, horror indeed, at an assumed relationship between Jean-Yves and myself; the fact that such a young cyclist should be in the company of an old woman. There was a lot of the Vietnamese equivalent of *'nudge nudge, wink wink'*. Had we been cycling around the Isle of Wight, the reaction might well have been the same, but at least the explanation of our chance meeting would, at the very least, have been understood and, hopefully, accepted. The limitations of sign language make this impossible so we suffered endless giggling and pointing, always from men. Jean-Yves appeared untroubled, giving a mere Gallic shrug of his shoulders. I, on the other hand, was enraged and could have cheerfully slapped those smirking faces.)

To reach the Chinese border, I still have several days of cycling and the strangest thing happens. All the aggression and hassling by the entire Vietnamese population ceases and is replaced with gentle and friendly curiosity – back to normal in other words. The reasons will never be known but the fact that I am again 'solo' cannot be entirely dismissed.

The border post is impressive and enough to set the pulse racing. Leaving Vietnam is done amidst stern and seemingly accusing looks from the armed officers, and having crossed over, the Chinese reaction is more, much more of the same. This does not feel good and I have to concentrate on trying not to smile – it is evident that smiles are not appreciated nor reciprocated.

As a supplement to Asia Overland I am also armed with a couple of photocopied pages from the French Lonely Planet. Vital questions are covered, such as *'Where can I buy an umbrella?'* (not kidding – they are used by everybody in Asia, including policemen, to provide protection more from the sun than rain) but the phrase *'When do I get out of jail?'* is not amongst them.

All preconceptions about China vanish within the first day. My expectations did not fall into the realms of hand drawn rickshaws, old men with spindly beards and pigtails, and women with bound feet, but I am quite unprepared for the fact that it is far from a third world country. It seems more like America than America, with huge cities, huge buildings, office blocks with red, green or blue reflective glazing, massive highways and traffic lights that count down the seconds until the red light changes to green. There are more bicycles than the most fertile imagination could conjure up and just as many motorbikes and scooters.

My reception on the road is utterly wonderful and such a welcome surprise. Every passing vehicle wants to show encouragement. This is always done with a grin and a *'thumbs up'*. (So much for the concern about lack of mutually understood sign language.) Men in trucks lean out of windows, those on motorbikes or scooters risk falling off as they look over their shoulder and wobble precariously, and cyclists draw alongside, unable to talk but just happy to be with me

The sight of an old woman on a bicycle with a heavy load is nothing unusual in China. It's what everybody's grandmother does. What they find incomprehensible is that it is a recreational choice. The bicycle in Asia is equivalent to a donkey with wheels and nobody pedals either downhill or quickly.

I stay in cheap hotels all the way to Hong Kong and the standard of the room varies from absolutely disgusting (but always with clean sheets which was not the case in India) to modern and immaculate. Without fail I would always find the following: television, thermos of hot water, tea bags, flip flops, a disposable toothbrush, toothpaste and a comb. And there is no truth in the rumour about loo paper, but as the toilet is in the same room as the shower it is often sodden and useless.

The need to track down accommodation encourages cunning tactics and I develop various strategies when hitting the outskirts of large towns. A particularly productive ruse is to ask in car showrooms. Amongst the large number of educated staff someone always speaks English and with a lack of customers and a degree of boredom, they are eager to help. (Other benefits are that the showrooms are always air conditioned and iced drinks available.)

Petrol stations also prove invaluable, again with several staff mostly unoccupied and keen to do their best but without the bonus of speaking English. When it becomes clear that I can't understand what they are saying, they repeat the words more slowly; and again even more slowly, each time moving a bit closer. Finally they write the message down and show it to me, on the basis that it will immediately become clear! This happens dozens of times, not just in petrol stations but many different shops. Endearing and frustrating in equal proportions. Sometimes I just stop at a street corner, often amongst the motorbike taxies, bring out the highlighted phrases and hope for the best.

Each day is about improvisation and trust which bring remarkable results.

In Zhanjian all efforts to find a hotel have failed with a great deal of time wasted going left and right, backwards and forwards, when I miraculously stumble on *'Chinese Tourism'* – a small place tucked in amongst the many shops. Stepping through that door changes the next three days. Two of the girls speak a bit of English and are keen to hear my story while I drink tea and eat the buns which someone has gone out to buy. They telephone around for a hotel negotiating a special rate and one of the lads leads me to it in due course. In the meantime, Li calls her brother, Jason, who works for the Immigration Police and he turns up on his motorbike. Because of my paranoia about not getting lost on the roads out of large towns or cities, he insists I jump on the pillion seat. He then rides the route so that I will know the way when the time comes, thus removing all anxiety.

Li and Jason are adamant that I should not leave the following morning and to ensure that I don't, Jason pays my hotel bill for the next three nights – he will have no argument. In the evening they organise a magnificent meal in the private room of a restaurant and we are joined by three other young couples. As it is Li's twenty first birthday next day, she invites me to spend it with her and a group of friends. The day is filled with tasty and extraordinary food, interspersed with a varied cocktail of sightseeing around the city, using several different types of transport. We travel in taxis, where the driver's seat is surrounded by a metal cage; very modern buses with music and air conditioning; and a bicycle rickshaw (no gears) with five of us on board – that poor man.

The highlight of the following day is when they take me to their parents' apartment for lunch. (The father has taken the afternoon off so that he can be present.) The food for nine people is spectacular and plentiful and has been cooked in what would be considered cupboard space in a Western house. Apart from masses of rice, twelve other dishes appear, half of which are fish and shell fish. (The greatest test of chop stick skills, apart from eating peanuts and slippery noodles, is to dissect fish which is served up completely in tact and then get it into your mouth without losing it several times.) As neither parent speaks English it is mortifying not to be able adequately to convey my appreciation and gratitude. I feel so privileged.

En route to Zhanjian there had been a puzzling intrusion into my hotel room in Lianzhu. I opened the door to insistent knocking, as I thought it was the girl returning to check if the replacement television was working. Instead, it was a man carrying a towel and gesturing frantically, gestures that could only be interpreted as washing hair – his or mine? As neither seemed a good idea, I shut and locked the door. He protested loudly with more unrelenting knocking and very stupidly I risked opening the door again. More miming, but this time of washing not just hair but the entire body. I don't think so. After slamming the door I was then left to worry about any repercussions concerning Alchemy, locked up very high profile in a public area on the ground floor. Would he seek revenge and reduce my precious bicycle to scrap metal; or slash the tyres perhaps?

Shortly after I checked into the hotel in Zhanjian there was intensive knocking. I opened the door, this time to find a woman. She was a complete stranger, not part of my newly found friends nor a member of the hotel staff, and was very smartly dressed in black evening clothes. It was impossible to discover what was on her agenda but she was absolutely furious when I refused to let her come in.

So, when on the evening of Li's birthday, there is more knocking on my door I am wondering just who I might find this time. Is there some quaint Chinese custom that the guide book has failed to mention? I certainly hadn't come across the phrase *'I have no idea what you want, but this is my room so will you kindly go away'* (or words to that effect). I had returned to the hotel, leaving Li celebrating with her friends and had settled down for the night. Then I hear Jason's voice.

'Are you tired Pam, or would you like to come out and play?'

Is it possible that I have lived to hear these words from a twenty five year old Chinese immigration officer?

'My friends are at a restaurant. The night life in China is great. They are excited to meet you. Will you come?'

It is tempting to refuse. I don't quite see myself fitting in with a bunch of young Chinese men out clubbing. But no, it turns out to be his aunt and a female cousin and we join them in another private room, this one part of a huge hotel complex. (These rooms are geared entirely to eating and they seem to be nothing extravagant or out of the ordinary.) A wonderful and never ending range of food is delivered on trolleys along with oceans of tea as we sit and chat with Jason acting as a competent interpreter.

'They are very proud of you' he tells me as my story unfolds.

It sums up the reaction I receive throughout the whole Chinese experience. Undiluted and open admiration, eagerness to share and help. Friendly but never intrusive curiosity.

I had suggested to Jason that I would prefer not to be back later than midnight. As the time approaches he looks at me and says 'It's OK for you to go.' This saves me either the embarrassment of having to ask or otherwise the irritation of having to stay longer than I want. Considerate and impressive.

Back at the hotel there is yet another visitor to my room, more difficult to identify as it didn't need to knock – it could scurry under the door. By now ready for much needed sleep, there is a disturbing and loud rustling in the polythene bags which contain my ever present picnic. Mice, rats – horrors. After turning on the light and shaking all the contents on to the bed, it is only the polythene that has been destroyed. The food remains untouched – how odd is that?

Ironically, attacking the food would have been preferable – it at least is replaceable. The carrier bags are not. Hoarded from European supermarkets they are playing a vital part in transporting my meals on wheels. These heavy gauge carrier bags are more than a rare commodity in Asia – they are unobtainable. I re-arrange everything and hang the contents in one bag on Alchemy's handlebar. At least the beast will need excellent gymnastic skills to forage again. Within a remarkably short period of time I hear more persistent rustling. Somehow clapping my hands and shouting seems feeble defence, but what else can I do? Sleep is now out of the question so I turn the light back on and the marauder is identified. It is the tiniest of lizards – about two to three inches long including its tail. They have been around as long as the mosquitoes; always on the walls of bedrooms and very shy – normally. This one must be addicted to polythene and realises what a treat he has in the special European vintage.

Back on the road again it is early afternoon and I am concerned about the distance to the next town. (Lucky to have found a bi-lingual map at all, it has a tiny scale which makes judging mileage almost impossible. Jean-Yves was unable to find such a map for south central China, so the one he bought had only Chinese script and it was impossible to tell whether or not it was upside down.) Cycling past a factory in the middle of nowhere, it feels right to go in and ask. The woman at the desk sits me down with a glass of much appreciated chilled water and then vanishes. When she reappears, she is carrying two large bowls: one full of the very wet rice that the Chinese seem to favour and the other full of sprouts and pork. Having demolished this, I am given a second helping. She encourages me to rest for a while and when I decide to move on an hour later there is a group of thirty men gathered outside in the car park to wave goodbye. I cannot understand a word that any of them are saying but it becomes clear that they are keen to establish my home country as they begin to draw pictures of flags in the dust! Such are the far reaching powers of the Olympic Games – recently held in Sydney.

It is about now that a certain irony strikes me. Before leaving England I purchased some highly recommended multi vitamin pills and decided that these should be saved until I reached China, having envisaged a poor diet, deprived of essential daily fruit and vegetables. As the jewel in my journey for so many reasons, China heads the list of countries where these two categories of food are most readily available, most tasty and extremely cheap. Nevertheless, I swallow one every day – if only to get rid of them from the luggage. One hundred pills worth of extra space....

Some days later I am standing amongst a gathering crowd in Jianchen when a girl passing on a scooter decides to stop. On hearing my English she intervenes and invites me to follow her. Once again I have stumbled upon someone who speaks English. She negotiates a phenomenally cheap rate of fifteen yen at a hotel and wanting to show my gratitude, I offer to buy her dinner this evening. But no, and as so often on the journey so far, a complete stranger takes control. Realising that I would be hungry, she disappears and returns shortly with a steaming hot meal of rice and pork with a delicious sauce all wrapped in a banana leaf. She then takes my cycling clothes home to wash. I have been in the town less than an hour and already experienced a genuine Chinese take away and genuine Chinese laundry.

Leaving me to have a sleep, she collects me later to eat dinner at her parents' home. Her father sells shoes on the pavement outside his front door and the entire tiny living room is stacked high with thousands of pairs. The dinner is a feast fit for royalty – surely a month's food budget has been blown in my honour. Afterwards she takes me for a tour around the city on the back of her scooter. Much to my delight and surprise, her brother owns a computer shop where I am able to send an email back home. Her consideration knows no bounds. She buys a dozen postcards of her city, as well as the stamps, aware that these add a special flavour and dimension for those receiving them and is proud to know that they will be going to my family and friends back in England. Still not finished, she drives me around a grid locked city centre, where we park the scooter and check out the hectic market stalls and shops all open in spite of the fact that it is ten o'clock. En route back to the hotel she insists on stopping for tea at a beautifully appointed restaurant where everything from sweet to savoury, cold to freshly cooked food is on offer – a never ending phalanx of trolleys laden with unbelievable choices is paraded past each table. All I can do is ask her to choose. Amongst the selection are some small white bony objects that looked remarkably like hen's feet – they are. Nothing of any animal gets wasted in this country so I take a nervous bite but have to resort to spitting most of it out, with an apology.

The culture of eating in China bears no resemblance to visiting a Chinese restaurant in England. It doesn't end with skills in using chopsticks. Spitting, sucking teeth and burping all play a big part and are very disconcerting if you have been brought up to believe that all these habits are bad manners. Indeed, spitting is an art form and whereas Westerners would remove a bone by using their fingers, in China the custom is to spit it out. Hands never touch food; they are only used to knock swiftly on the table to indicate the wish for more tea when it is offered. (It was in Vietnam that I had been physically repelled by spitting of Olympic standards. Jean-Yves and I had stopped at a roadside restaurant. At a nearby table a dozen men were eating lunch and by the time they had finished not only was the table covered with food that had been spat out, but also the floor.)

But the spitting out of food out is only part of the whole story. Both men and women spit publicly anywhere and everywhere. It is as integral to life as breathing – compulsory perhaps – especially walking on crowded pavements, but also out of the windows of vehicles (unwelcome if you're on a bike). There is the silent gentle variety (as if the perpetrator can't be bothered to swallow accumulated saliva) which slips quietly out of the mouth and plops on the pavement; then there is the stomach churning audible variety preceded by extensive throat clearing and ejected with a guttural hawk (the noisy preamble at least gives you a chance of side stepping the resulting missile). One example of how unfazed the Chinese are by this habit will surely suffice. Having checked into a hotel, I was invited to join a large family gathering in their living room. A man in his twenties was sitting on the sofa and he gobbed right there on the floor next to the table where food was spread. I did my very best not to flinch and definitely didn't look. Nobody else appeared to notice, or clear it up.

Combined with spitting is nose picking. It could be described as an art form and is also done very publicly. During this same scene a young teenage boy, leaning up against the spitter, picked his nose with concentrated intensity for several minutes.

There are many other idiosyncratic habits that are more endearing. The fingernails of many of the men are of claw like proportions. Often only on one hand and equally often only the thumb and first finger. It is impossible to fathom out the reason, any more than I never discover just why so many men roll up just one of their trouser legs or the body section of their shirt – bizarre but very widespread. Another frequent sight is a scrap of tissue stuck on a man's face. As a race who have little or no body hair perhaps it is a status symbol – as in 'I needed to shave this morning'.

Other sights are more familiar and easy to understand. I have been thrilled to see Chinese men playing Chinese Chequers and Mah Jong – two beloved childhood games. When cycling out of towns in the early morning I usually see groups of older men playing badminton either on the pavement or in a square. And without fail both morning and evening I come across men and women exercising, usually in a park, sometimes led by music as part of a group, sometimes quietly on their own.

It is while cycling that I witness the most astonishing sight. It is in a town early in the morning where stalls are being set up on the pavements and there are plenty of people around. In the middle of the road is a totally naked woman holding a whip which she uses to herd a single buffalo. She is behaving completely naturally and nobody (other than myself) is taking any notice. Common sense tells me that the temptation to take a photograph must be resisted. Then, two days later and eighty miles further on I come across an identical scene. An extraordinary diversion.

A much less welcome spectacle is when meals on wheels take on a new dimension. Towed on a trailer behind a bicycle are six live ducks, squished into a cement bag with their heads sticking out of individually cut holes, three either side. The first time I came across this atrocity, I had been aware of insistent quacking in the distance and made the mistake of looking up hoping to see a formation fly past. But no, the swooshing of wings was absent as these ducks were reluctant passengers and the sound was that of their protests. I have plenty of time to reflect on whether or not this was more cruel than the transport of live chickens used back home.

Another lasting memory while cycling between towns was the alternate style of highway maintenance. On several occasions I witnessed dozens of men squatting alongside the road, each tapping away with a hammer and chisel. Like the ducks, you could hear them long before you could see them and they too had all arrived by bicycle. In a different way, it reminded me of a visit to a busy restaurant in Delhi. Men were employed on each of its three crowded floors as well as at the entrance, their sole purpose being to clean the carpet with a dustpan and brush. They too squatted silently as they moved between people's legs carrying out their task without pause.

156

There is no finer example of synchronicity than in Foshan. I have wandered into the car park of a very expensive modern hotel and am contemplating whether I have the nerve to ask if they could recommend a cheap alternative when a voice drifts over the hedge from the pavement.

'Hello. Are you looking for something? Is there anything that I can do to help?'

It is Van who has seized the moment as he walks by and yet again I am hijacked in the most exquisite style for the next few days. First, he finds an excellent hotel nearby where he persuades the two sisters who own it to knock the price down from eighty yen to fifty yen.

He suggested to them 'This is an extraordinary opportunity to have a very important visitor staying in your hotel. She is a lady from England who is travelling through China on a bicycle.'

He is twenty two and extremely proud of his city which we spend a couple of days cycling around. The time flies by with a perfect combination of sightseeing (including a two thousand year old temple, the ancient home and gardens belonging to past governors of this area and, as stark contrast, a modern four storey library) interspersed with plenty of delicious food.

It is during this tour of the city that Alchemy's back tyre decides to disintegrate, so the moment has arrived for the £2 spare to earn its keep. Can it really be a coincidence that this has happened in the presence of a young man who owns a mountain bike (not just rare in China but the only one I saw throughout the entire Asian continent) and is familiar with handling derailleur gears? Not only does Van know exactly how to tackle the replacement but his sense of chivalry persuades me to take the role of spectator – he doesn't want me to get my hands dirty! It seems that my misgivings of not having joined an evening class on bicycle maintenance are ill founded.

One evening the two sisters invite us out for a magnificent dinner during which Van does an excellent job as interpreter. This cannot be easy but he never fails to make sure that the three of us feel included and his English is so good that he is able to pick up on nuances and humour.

For instance, I tell them 'I could never have found the hotel that the sisters run by myself. Apart from the fact that it is up two flights of stairs and behind a locked door, it is impossible for me to recognise a hotel sign in this country. Because the letters '*h o t e l*' are never used, which is not the case in say Vietnam, they are difficult to spot if you don't understand the Chinese script.'

Van replies 'You have to understand, Pam, that as in English you have different words for a place where you can book accommodation, so it is in Chinese. You don't just use hotel do you? There are other words: inn, guest house, bed and breakfast, lodge, tavern, pub.'

The staggering fact is that he has never spoken English to anyone before – his knowledge has been gained solely within a classroom.

His sensitivity and thoughtfulness don't end there. The next stage of my route will incur the alarming prospect of negotiating my way through Dongguan, a vast city. I hadn't voiced my apprehensions to Van but realising the enormity of the challenge ahead, he has opted to take the day off work, explaining the situation to his boss.

'It would be helpful for the goodwill between our two countries.'

Whatever this young man does for a living, he is wasted. He should be with the United Nations.

The only moment of drama is when one of the pedals on his bike falls off and with a very worn thread and no tools, finding someone to put it back tests even his ingenuity and determination. By the time he returns home he would have covered more miles than I, but his tiredness would be compensated by the fact that he was very aware of just how much I had valued his company and compassion.

As always in life there is a balance and there is one evening when the goodwill and kindness are replaced by a blatant rip off. Everything started well in Diancheng, a much smaller and less affluent town. A woman left her stall to walk me through a maze of tiny streets and dilapidated buildings to find a very primitive guest house. When she took me up several flights of stairs to find the man in charge, we interrupted a large male gathering and I was the centre of much laughter and pointing. The Team was carried up the stairs and the price agreed at twenty yen. I locked myself in a huge and disgusting room and had a 'shower' – an elaborate description of the plumbing that allowed cold water to escape from a pipe sticking out of the wall in full view of the street below, as the plain glass windows had no curtains. It was then mid-afternoon so I fell asleep.

Around six o'clock there is loud and insistent knocking. This is the owner indicating that he will take me over the road to get a meal. Excellent – local food at local prices. Several men accompany us, all sitting around one table and there is a great deal of hilarity as they check out my photocopied phrases and the China section of my travel book, along with the map showing my route. Nobody speaks any English but the atmosphere is full of the Chinese equivalent of 'bon homie'. The eating place is primitive with limited cooking facilities and no choice, so I am given cold rice with cold chicken (half a cooked carcass coarsely hacked into pieces) and some greens. Everybody tucks in and even with my now highly improved chopstick skills less than half of the food finds its way into my mouth. I am getting a strong feeling about the outcome of all this – I am to be the involuntary and reluctant benefactor. The assembled group encourage me to order the same again and in a half hearted attempt to make my point, I indicate that I don't want any more. It is at their instigation that the second helping arrives and it is also they who consume the lot. Accompanying the food, a very potent liquor is being liberally poured and drunk. I have had a sip and nearly choked, much to the delight of my companions. It is disgusting and they are drinking it as if it were beer.

Considering the standard of food eaten in China up to this point, this meal is as revolting as the surroundings which could be symbolically and literally summed up at the moment when one of the men picks up a plastic stool and hurls it across the room at a rat. Very keen to leave, I am not surprised when I am presented with the bill for the entire meal; what is so shocking is that it is three times more expensive than the best of food that I have eaten in wonderful and meticulous surroundings – often two or three courses, hot and freshly cooked. I am absolutely furious.

I have eaten several times on my own and the way this works is to find a restaurant, go to the fridges in the kitchen, choose which fish to have and then select the vegetables to go with it. A particularly memorable moment came when I opted for squid. I looked to the girl for guidance in choosing one of many unidentifiable greens to accompany it into the sizzling wok. Agreeing with her one suggestion, I then pointed to a couple more – not unreasonable for one who loves vegetables. The girl looked at me in total shock and horror and her colleague echoed the reaction. One needed no common language to understand that my choice symbolised a culinary crime. The looks said it all. *'What – red pepper with squid? You cannot be serious.'*

I commit a similar transgression eating one evening on my own in a cosy small restaurant. The son of the owner, a student at the local university, is sitting with me keen to practise his English and has also advised me about choice of food. The rice, whether it is the wet variety or the more customary dry rice we are used to, is always served separately and when it arrives I pour a liberal quantity of soy sauce all over it, only to look up and see a look of absolute dismay on his face. I can only apologise as I have obviously offended his gastronomic sensibilities.

My last meal in China has memories of a different kind. The fish are not neatly tucked up in a large fridge in the kitchen. Instead they are crammed into a couple of fish tanks in the same room that the customers eat in. Having sat down, I confirm that I want to eat and before I have any inkling of what is about to happen, an inmate of one of the tanks is in the wok having been chopped into several pieces. There is a degree of comfort drawn from the fact that the tanks are so disgracefully restricted, shallow and gaspingly over populated that during my meal one of his colleagues makes a suicidal leap on to the floor. This bore the desperate message that if the wok is inevitable it might as well come sooner rather than later.

Chapter Twenty

Getting out of China and into Hong Kong develops into an unexpected nightmare. Shenzen, the border town, has two crossing points. One is by train on which bicycles are banned. The second point is by road – from which bicycles are also banned. (I am blissfully unaware of this absurdity until events unravel and anyway, how can this be justified where the bicycle is such an integral part of the fabric of the country? It is another clue as to how Hong Kong and China are really about as integrated as Mars and Venus.)

When I arrive at Customs at seven o'clock in the morning several officials scratch their heads in bewilderment. The problem: what to do with The Team? Challenged by angry policemen about my presence in the car/coach park, they end up smiling and doing their best to help, with the result that passing through Chinese Emigration is straightforward. The drama starts when I set off to cycle the three miles of no-man's land – the road which leads to Hong Kong Immigration. For an agonising period it seems as if this is where my days might end. It is beyond the bounds of the bureaucratic imagination that I should be allowed to cycle. (Why? It is just a road.)

The only alternative is by bus but an officious woman on duty informs me that bicycles are not allowed on the public buses and in all seriousness, suggests that the only option is to throw myself at the mercy of the private tour coaches and try to hitch a lift! Determined not to panic, I explain the conundrum to a young policewoman in the Customs Hall who speaks fluent English and her reaction is spectacularly helpful, because not only does she understand my distress but she takes control of the dilemma and resolves it with several phone calls. In the meantime she explained to me what she intended to do which allowed me to sit quietly and calm down. The compromise she arranges is that once the initial morning rush of workers has subsided, The Team could board a bus with school children, who are thrilled at the curious passenger, and to pacify the stroppy Job's Worth, two tickets for the journey are purchased – one for me and one for the bicycle.

I am genuinely upset at saying goodbye to China – the outstanding gem in the journey.

(Since returning it has been possible to understand the background to my extraordinary reception. My route to Hong Kong was through the industrial south east of China along main roads and through huge cities, an area which has no history or scenery to lure tourists or backpackers, so my presence offered a unique opportunity for those bold enough to seize it. And the reason it was always twenty somethings who approached me is because they are the first generation who have had the opportunity to learn English at school. For those who had been paying attention, they had a sound basic knowledge of the language but had never before had the chance of speaking it outside the classroom. I was the live guinea pig. It also ensured a unique perspective of a country which, had I visited the Great Wall and other such attractions, could never have occurred. The other enormous stroke of luck was that Jean-Yves had wanted to accompany me to Hong Kong before heading up to Beijing, but needed a double entry visa to do so. It is worth a reminder here that China and Hong Kong are supposed to be integrated but by 'leaving' China to visit Hong Kong, the single entry does not allow the traveller to return. By the time he realised this he had already secured a single entry and was not prepared to pay the extra. Although it did not feel like it at the time, it very quickly became apparent that this was a huge stroke of good fortune for me – solo again – whew. To have been denied all this interaction with the wonderful people who sought me out in south east China would have been catastrophic. Whew again.)

The swift three mile bus ride transports me to all intents and purposes half way around the world. Cycling on the left hand side has been expected, but it is the overall format of everything to do with the road system that comes as such a surprise – a replica of England. I might have been back in Sussex. Gone too is the recently familiar traffic of bicycles, rickshaws, scooters and motorbikes, along with the friendly greetings and welcome curiosity. The Chinese in Hong Kong appear to be doing everything in their power not to be Chinese. This is particularly reflected by the women whose hair is so frequently died and permed; and gone are those ten storey high platform shoes. And no more spitting.... there are compensations.

The climax to the day comes as I soar, both emotionally and physically, down a hill with Hong Kong harbour spread out before me. This is a breathtaking and colossal landmark in every sense. Never had I imagined that I would visit Hong Kong and here I am – arriving on a bicycle. Indeed a moment to savour but taking care at the same time not to get squished by the traffic.

The plan is to head straight for the RSA offices as they are expecting me. Gavin, my son, had arranged for two spare tyres to be couriered there and it is very much hoped that someone will have some guidance on accommodation. To get there I have the thrill of crossing the harbour on a ferry (having first had to find which would carry a bicycle – no surprise by now), followed by a nerve wracking ride amongst traffic travelling at turbo charged speeds. Am I the first bicycle ever in this city? It certainly feels like it because my presence is definitely resented. As if to prove the point, I am steadily cycling along tucked in to the side of the road when a taxi hits the outside back pannier causing Alchemy to lurch forward involuntarily and wobble violently but somehow I manage not to fall off. The driver must have been braking hard in an effort to avoid me and the next thing is the sound of crunching metal as a bus runs into the back of his taxi. I do stop to witness the scene and hear the sound of raised and angry voices but then have no compunction in continuing on my way. Nobody has been hurt and my only crime was being there.

After my four previous hospitable receptions from RSA offices, the Hong Kong version is a huge contrast – nobody is quite sure what to do with me as I definitely make the place look untidy. To have followed up their leads on hotels, one would have needed a lavish expense account, so after demolishing two very necessary mugs of tea and sending an email update back home, I collect my parcel and leave. My reliable Asia Overland has low budget choices, but instead I follow advice from a couple on the ferry. A big mistake, as it turns out. By the time I return to Kowloon, it is dark. This is a first for me, incorporating all my nightmares – evening, nowhere to sleep, in the middle of a huge, unfamiliar and very expensive city.... with a bicycle. The couple suggested the YMCA, which sounded an eminently sensible and cheap idea. But in Hong Kong they fall into the same category as expense account hotels – HK$550 (£50).

The fiasco to find somewhere else within my budget takes on the form of an uncoordinated treasure hunt. The YMCA porter suggests a cheap hotel nearby.

'It is on the left and only five minutes down the road' he tells me.

(This information is hopeless – would that be *'pedestrian'* or *'bus'* minutes? Certainly not *'cycling'* minutes – not in Hong Kong.)

Seeing no sign of any hotel, I stick my head into a restaurant to ask for help. A customer who is about to leave overhears and everyone agrees they know of no such place. However, he has another idea. He not only leads me to a hotel but then insists on accompanying me to the fifth floor in a lift which is so minuscule that Alchemy has to be upended – a significant achievement with all four panniers still attached – only to discover that the primary function of this place is that of intimate romantic encounters. The rooms are let out by the hour and business must have been brisk because we are told that one would not be available for the night until eleven o'clock. The comparatively good news is that it will cost a mere HK$200 but it is only six o'clock which means five hours of hanging around. And anyway, do I really want to sleep in a giant heart shaped bed swamped with ribbons and violent pink décor, besieged by images of the activities of the past several hours? I think not. By enormous good fortune the first five minutes of time killing draws me past the YWCA, cheaper by HK$200 than its male counterpart. A treat at this stage does not seem unreasonable, so the credit card is dusted off and the power shower turned on.

With several thousand miles under the pedals, it seems wise to find an expert to give Alchemy some tlc. A lucky stab in the yellow pages results in the perfect greasy spanner bike shop. It is a bit of a Catch 22 as the bicycle had been performing perfectly, apart from a clicking pedal.

Pushing my technical jargon to the limit I suggest 'This bicycle has travelled a very long way so perhaps it would be sensible to replace the chain. Can you tell by looking at it whether it needs changing?'

The lad who is serving me says 'I think it's best to leave it alone. It looks in perfect condition and there is a real risk that if you change one thing there will be a knock-on effect with other moving parts and you might find some miles down the road suddenly everything grinds to a halt.'

He does do me the huge service of packing the bicycle in a box ready for the flight across the Pacific in a way that no amount of flight changes or handling could destroy. It is in this shop that I buy the CatEye computer with tendencies to hypothermia.

The only decision now is where next: Canada, California or Mexico, so I spend time doing some homework by browsing in a bookshop. My geography for the Americas' stage is vague and with the money that Hong Kong is costing, indecision is a luxury I cannot afford.

Top: Breakfast with Jean-Yves, Laos
Bottom: Audience during lunch, Laos

Top: Televisions in transit, Vietnam
Bottom: Waiting at traffic lights, Hanoi

Top: Duck cargo, China
Bottom: Companions in the park, China

*Top:*Motorway maintenance, China
Bottom: Van, my guide, China

Top: Chinese motorway
Bottom: Ferry across to Hong kong

Top: Totonac Indian display, Mexico
Bottom: Play area, part of church facilities, America

AMERICA

Chapter Twenty

Because I have vastly overestimated the cost of travelling through the Asian countries, there is a fistful of dollars in my luggage rather larger than feels wise to carry any further. Eager to pay this cash back into my account, I am standing outside Citibank half an hour before it opens. The number of security guards also taking up space on the steps and on the pavement is sufficient to make up a private army and their collection of high profile hardware is intimidating – the sort that could never be mistaken as a cigarette lighter or plastic toy. But my mission is in vain. As these dollars were withdrawn from my account in a bank in Bangkok, it did not seem unreasonable to assume that they could be repaid through a bank in Mexico City. The woman the other side of the glass fails to understand my request, as do all of her colleagues who have joined in the fun. Something might be missing in the translation, or more accurately total lack of any. The special needs of this transaction stretch way beyond the limitations of sign language, so the dollars are replaced in the money belt around my waist. With the surplus of guards outside, perhaps one would prefer to accompany me to protect my surplus of cash, if he has the inclination and a bicycle.

A significant incident occurred this morning which demonstrated how continued warnings about danger can unwittingly get into your head and influence behaviour. It is my second day in Mexico City and I had set off early to have breakfast before going to the bank. Part of the walk was through a large park, deserted at that time of day. A man approaching me slowed and started to speak. Very aware of the bulging money belt, I bowed my head and walked faster, ensuring that no eye contact was made and cursing myself for being so stupid as to go through an empty park, when sticking to the roads would have been an easy option. Then I heard him shouting and instinctively I stopped and turned around. He too had stopped and was walking in my direction. Adrenaline flooded through my body and my heart was racing. But instead of the anticipated attack, it became very clear that he was genuinely upset. He indicated that all he wanted to do was say hello, and then doubtless check on my age. I felt ashamed. How grateful I was that this *'don't talk to strangers'* attitude had not permeated the rest of my journey.

It is during the couple of days walking around that I discover the Volkswagen beetle is very much alive and well. There are thousands of them in Mexico City where they have adopted the communal role of city taxis and are all painted green and white.

The time has now come to set off into the unknown sierras of Mexico. Would there be a bandit behind every cactus or would it be safer riding Alchemy than travelling in a bus? Buses are subject to regular highway robberies because the rewards are rich pickings for the least amount of effort. Why mug a single person when you can knock off a whole bus load of passengers? From the sheer volume, intensity and speed of traffic, the ride on main roads to Jalapa appeared terrifying enough just viewed through the windows of the bus and this was sufficient to encourage risking the cross country route. As it turns out, the choice made from ignorance and a small scale map proves an excellent one.

Leaving the exhaust fumes behind and hindered from in front by a beastly headwind, the entire morning is spent in the granny gear grinding relentlessly uphill, but the scenery makes the effort worthwhile. The mountains are stunning, the traffic nil, the temperature now only twenty something. My fitness level combined with the gradient and the excellent road surface means that I can revel in my surroundings and appreciate my extreme good fortune. Nevertheless half an hour after midday (five and a half hours of cycling) only thirty five miles have been covered and my destination is at least as far again. As there is no clue about the uphill challenge ever ending, getting nowhere other than tired seems more and more likely.

It's time to stop and have what the Mexicans laughingly call coffee. Referred to as café con latté, it is a strange concoction of concentrated instant coffee where an egg cupful is tipped into a glass and topped up with luke warm milk. The resulting drink is barely coffee and barely warm. Succeeding only in colouring the milk but adding no flavour, there is little danger of a caffeine fix here. The humidity is so high that a newly opened packet of biscuits becomes soggy in less than ten minutes.

Will it be possible to arrive at my destination before darkness threatened? Always my worst nightmare. Definitely not at this rate and worse still, ominous black clouds are gathering. Then suddenly, without warning, the reward. My conviction that this is Mexico's rival to Everest is joyfully disproved when a hundred yards beyond the coffee stop all pedalling ceases and amidst swirling mist The Team swoops downhill for the next thirty five miles. Freedom, speed, leaning into corners, flying down straights – no need for caffeine. This buzz is infinitely more stimulating.

Suddenly out of nowhere a dog gives chase and the adrenaline rush is topped up by fear. For a cyclist, man's best friend transforms into a snarling and threatening carnivore. Unless tethered or constrained by a fence, the dog will run close alongside snapping and barking. Sensing juicy calves and a heel bone to gnaw on, they are terrifying because they mean serious business. This is not the first time I've been attacked and those bulky back panniers have always prevented the predator from drawing blood. But this large Mexican mongrel has a different tactic. He sinks his jaws into one of the panniers and performs a perfect cartoon re-enactment of desperately trying to screech to a halt. The bike slows dramatically and I am forced to pedal like mad. But sensing succulent flesh and being rewarded with a mouthful of black canvas, he redoubles his efforts and tries again and again before eventually giving up. Prior to leaving England I very reluctantly spent £100 on a rabies vaccination and with the speed that one's mind can work on these occasions, it is not so much my life that flashes before me but a reflection on whether or not that money has been well invested. Had I been cycling up that hill I would probably have found out.

It gets no better than Mexico if you are a fruit addict. Part of my daily fix is citrus fruit because it is harvest time and the overfilled trucks shed hundreds of oranges, tangerines and grapefruit on the road side. Not only tasty and free, they are an excellent form of re-hydration and energy. In the towns there are stalls and shops which sell only fruit based drinks. Every imaginable blend is chucked into a liquidiser with ice or ice cream and because only seasonal fruit is used, the result is truly scrumptious – an addiction of the most healthy and mouth watering kind.

My evenings are spent wandering through a town, ending up always in the main square with its unique family atmosphere. Food stalls doing a roaring trade, young children in mini workshops making plaster casts and painting, teenagers parading, couples promenading hand in hand and older men and women dancing, blissfully content, to live music – everyone dressed in their best. And always the shoeshine boys doing a brisk trade.

Because my map is an absurdly tiny scale, it is impossible to judge exact distances between towns or precisely where I might be at any given point. Sometimes hot and exhausted and desperately willing the end of the ride, it becomes irresistible to stop and ask how much further to my destination. Compulsive but ill advised, the stupidity of this was learnt way back in Europe. Car drivers and pedestrians never have a clue of precise distance, which is usually judged in time – *'about an hour'* or *'ten minutes away'*. When each mile is hurting this is not what you want to hear. On one particularly gruelling ride I stupidly choose to stop three times within about as many minutes to ask the futile question. The answers given by three separate people within a space of a couple of hundred meters are *'sixteen'*, *'twenty six'* and *'thirty six kilometres'*! Why ask at all? Well, somehow the pain and fading energy are much easier to deal with if the precise extent of the challenge is known.

One picturesque day The Team detours along the coast to a busy fishing town for a memorable breakfast on the beach. Heading back inland along fifteen miles of unforgiving track (potholes separated by boulders or is it the other way around), my lunch (always a hugely anticipated, never mind essential refuelling moment of each day) is destroyed. At the market earlier this morning I treated myself to a giant, ripe avocado and the continuous bumping and bouncing has reduced it to guacamole, skin and all, and salvaging even a mouthful is impossible. There must be limits as to how much roughage is acceptable.

Any idea of maintaining a rigid vegetarian diet was abandoned shortly after leaving England and therefore the prospect of eating at a dedicated vegetarian restaurant in Tampica has been eagerly looked forward to with drooling impatience, particularly in a country with such an abundance of fruit and vegetables. It is to be a rare treat. But this anticipation is quickly replaced with a bigger helping of disappointment. The salad consists of a meagre portion of cooked (and worse than cooked, *overcooked*) soggy and tasteless vegetables, accompanied by a couple of limp lettuce leaves and a single slice of tomato. The drink is a small glass of synthetic blackcurrant cordial. And the dessert – two slices of *tinned peaches*. The waiter presents the bill which puts me close to cardiac arrest – the cost of this diabolical travesty would buy fresh fruit, cheese and avocados for a month.

It is at this point that the proud owner approaches. 'Did you enjoy your meal?' she asks. 'It isn't often we get someone from England in here.' My sense of injustice and outrage overcomes any need to be polite.

'How can you possibly serve tinned peaches in the height of the season? Fresh fruit is so plentiful and is not just tasty, it is also really cheap. Anything out of tin in a restaurant is absolutely disgraceful. I could go so far as to say verging on criminal.'

'It is precisely because there is such an abundance of fresh fruit that we do this. Fresh fruit is nothing special here in Mexico. Available throughout the year it is taken for granted. On the other hand, tinned peaches are considered a real luxury' she explains.

Should I laugh or cry?

The major highlight of the ride north is a couple of days spent in Paplanta to visit the site of El Tajin. Having seen Aztec ruins on television, I am quite unprepared for the impact of being amongst them. Even with my unfertile imagination, it is difficult not to ponder on what life was like some 2000 years ago – all ritual, superstition and hard grind. It is important to climb to the top of the highest pyramid to take in the atmosphere and the view. The people who lived at the time must have had tiny feet as the steps are incredibly narrow. When I encounter a group of teenagers on their way down, a boy and a girl turn around and help me to the top!

Travelling to the ruins by local bus, I spot a touring bike parked up by the entrance. It is difficult to resist the childish urge to jump for joy. A rare breed – a fellow long distance cyclist. But where is he or she? Writing a note would be futile and any idea of hanging around for several hours would be ridiculous. Somewhat reluctantly I head off to explore the several acres of the site. Amongst the small scattering of sightseers is this skinny guy on his own and carrying none of the usual tourist baggage such as camera, backpack, water bottle, guide book.

It is with only slight hesitation that I approach him.

'Are you the owner of the touring bike at the entrance?' I ask.

He looks at me very suspiciously. 'Yes, I am. Why do you ask?'

'I am cycling through Mexico as well. Since leaving England I have only come across two other touring cyclists, one German and one Japanese. I couldn't resist the opportunity to come and find out.'

Frank is German and speaks fluent English and Spanish. His journey started in Canada and is destined to finish in the southern tip of South America. Unlike me he is a seasoned lone touring cyclist, incredibly relaxed and laid back and has specially learned to speak Spanish before leaving.

'With this trip in mind, I flew to Canada without a bicycle and managed to find a job in a bike shop. With the help and skill of the two guys who worked there, we made a bicycle more or less from spare parts and so not only is it the perfect bike for me, it cost me nothing and I earned good money during the few months that I worked there.' How about that for casual?

With much to talk about we spend the rest of the day and evening together. I am particularly keen to hear about his experiences cycling through America, perceived by many I had met en route as perhaps the most dangerous of all the countries on my itinerary (many of these warnings from none other than Americans).

'Part of my route was along the Mississippi always keeping off the main roads. The poverty is so shocking. Some parts have the feeling of a third world country. But even in these surroundings I was never threatened.'

Whilst Frank and I are picnicking on the lawn, a team of five Mexican Indians approach, curious about his bike and its four panniers. They are Totonacs and several times each day they perform a remarkable ceremony which starts with all five climbing up a thirty meter pole to the platform at the top. Whilst one sits in the centre banging on a drum and playing a flute, each of the other four wraps yards of rope around his waist and then they hurl themselves backwards off the platform which is now spinning and gradually spiral upside down to the ground. It is no less than a slow motion choreographed bungee jump. How can this ritual have come into being and what does it symbolise? It is an unique spectacle, so much so that this team travels around the world giving performances. They clearly could not arrive at the airport check in with the pole which would never pass as hand luggage and as a jumbo jet doesn't have a roof rack, we were intrigued to know how it was transported. Sawing it into sections didn't seem a very safe option. Apparently it is always made locally. The group had visited France and their unanimous and only observation on this country was that the food was boring and disgusting and the bread was rubbish. From the land where the tortilla rules....

While walking around Paplanta that evening, there is a public weighing machine standing on the pavement. Encouraged by Frank, not least because he could read the scales without glasses, I decide to blow one peseta to check my weight. Confident that there is less of me than when I set out, my suspicions are confirmed but I am shocked at just how much less – thirteen kilos. All my adult life I have clocked in at sixty five kilos which at five feet eight inches has felt more or less acceptable. This seems to put an end to any argument about whether or not calories and exercise are connected.

Chapter Twenty One

My destination is the US border at Matamoros which means psyching up for US immigration. There will be no need for a hot shower to get the blood pumping at seven o'clock this morning. How will the officials cope with a touring cyclist who has no plane ticket? My brother lives in Atlanta and his work, home and mobile telephone numbers are on stand by. And for the first time in this tale, there is no need to cut a long story short. Instead it will be necessary to make a short story long, because the whole episode is an anti climax – nothing happens.

It is important to explain that all road border crossings are confusing, not least of all because the authorities are never sure whether my bicycle and I qualify as a vehicle or as a pedestrian. Another dilemma is that it is impossible to know exactly when one country has been exited and the next one entered. Only in Hong Kong was the no-man's land so well defined. On this occasion, *'we'* are judged to be a vehicle and having crossed the bridge, a woman at the check point indicates that I should head for the three uniformed men standing in a parking area – the place where cars get disembowelled.

As I approach I enquire 'Which country am I in?'

'The good ol' US of A, ma'am – why do you ask?'

'Because I wasn't sure if I was still in Mexico. This is a serious landmark for me. The States is the last country on my journey.'

'What journey is that, ma'am?' one of them enquires.

'I started from England....' They are incredulous.

They are also not busy and I am very fearful that such a unique opportunity will prove more than they can resist –

belongings needlessly scattered (vivid flashbacks of Calcutta airport) and irrelevant delving questions.

'Do you have any fruit?' is the first. 'Does a water melon have pips?' I am tempted to reply but wise from past experiences, the inclination to be frivolous is suppressed.

'Well, yes, I do. I've got a banana, an orange, a pear and a bunch of grapes.'

'I regret to have to tell you that we have to confiscate all of them. It's illegal to bring any fruit into the country.'

I know that drug trafficking along the Mexican border is a problem, but fruit? 'It's my breakfast' I protest. 'I can eat it now and that will be the end of that. I get to have breakfast, the fruit isn't wasted and no laws are broken. After all, had I eaten it the other side of the bridge none of you would have been any the wiser. It's the same difference.'

'No, sorry ma'am, that's not an option. We can't allow you to do that. You'll have to hand it all over.' So I do. Perhaps my last pesetas would have been better spent on a can of peaches.

They cast their eyes eagerly over the four panniers and begin their search while I plead with them not to unpack everything. Surprisingly, they decide to co-operate and check only the contents of one of the small panniers. It is all quickly and painlessly over and I haul on a drawstring believing it to be the one which tightens the top of the pannier but no – this one is attached to the rape alarm. Had my intention been to make an unobtrusive entrance into the States, this was not the best way to go about it. The early morning peace is shattered and everybody leaps six feet in the air, not least of all me who has never had cause to use or even test it, so getting the pin back in and shutting down the racket takes an embarrassingly long time.

'Have you experienced any trouble while you've been riding through Mexico?' they are keen to find out, convinced they are about to be entertained by a succession of horror stories.

'Absolutely not, apart from one ill intentioned dog' I assure them.

'Really? Why that's unbelievable. Everyone knows that it's such a dangerous country and surely it's on odds-on certainty that a woman travelling on her own would be in constant danger.'

Nothing changes. That familiar bad neighbour theme again.

They then inform me I am free to go. 'What, that's it? What about my passport? Don't I get a stamp – something?' I ask.

'No, ma'am, it's not necessary. We're done. Have a nice day' is the reply.

'Are you quite sure?' I am very concerned – that strong gut feeling again. They have paid more attention to my fruit than my passport. Even in third world countries at the most primitive of border road crossings the normal procedure was high-tech computer scanning accompanied by long hard stares. So, I mount up and letting out a restrained squeal of deeply felt joy and relief, head north, chastising myself as always for so much unnecessary worry. But, within twenty four hours those instincts about it all being too easy would come back to haunt me.

I am in Brownsville, Texas with no idea of what lies ahead and the local Chamber of Commerce proves a wonderful source of free maps and other handy information. Because the staff quickly ascertain the background to my presence, I am asked to hang around while they organise interviews with the local radio, television and newspaper. The building is air conditioned and coffee and cookies are in plentiful supply. How can I refuse? The filter coffee is the first I've drunk since Austria and my body is struck by several volts of caffeine. And if this isn't enough to prove I'm back on western soil, the tentative approach to establishing my age is the final evidence.

'May we…. ?' 'Do you mind if…. ?' 'Would you be prepared to tell us…. ?'

It is also a reminder that I don't have to start each sentence with *'Do you speak English?'* All that sign language a thing of the past.

I am surprised at how exciting it feels to be in the States. Probably because it is the last country on the list – a realisation tinged with relief that I have got this far.

As the cost of even the cheapest motel is beyond my budget and campsites are several hundred miles apart, I intend to adopt a different strategy regarding accommodation at the end of each day's ride, namely to knock on the door of a private home and ask if I can pitch my tent in the garden (referred to as *'back yard'* by Americans). The principle is simple enough but I am feeling very apprehensive at the prospect. It had worked well enough as a one-off in France but in The States it is going to be on a daily basis. My fingers are very crossed.

My tactics are always the same. Ensuring that the bike with its four panniers is in full sight (which cuts down dramatically on explanations) my first words are along the lines of *'I have a very unusual request....'* I have convinced myself that at least as an older woman travelling alone I will represent less of a threat than, say, a teenage boy so the odds must be in my favour. My major selling point is to emphasise that I am entirely self contained (which is true) but would appreciate being able to use the bathroom.

In spite of several refusals, the first night is very encouraging. It is a household with three women at home who are trusting enough to agree. The odd thing is that my request has been answered 'Yes' and that was it. Not another word, never mind any questions. There is a nostalgic moment. When putting up the tent, an untouched part of the luggage since arriving in Pakistan, I discover grains of sand from a Turkish beach – not enough to make a castle but plenty to stir up memories. During the evening the daughter brings out a hot tasty meal which she delivers with a smile but in complete silence.

On day two in the States I am one hundred miles into Texas travelling north with only ranch land, cattle and cactus for company. The remoteness is confirmed by the fact that there hasn't been a McDonalds for the last fifty miles. Instead there is an isolated modern building which turns out to be US Border Patrol, a check point which has been strategically placed to round up drug smugglers or illegal immigrants just when they think that they've made it.

There are several cars in a queue but of course I am the only bicycle – not just today, probably ever. An armed officer approaches me.

'Good morning' I say chirpily, pleased to break my own silence, then add somewhat unnecessarily 'I've cycled up from Mexico and am headed to San Antonio.'

Clearly unimpressed or interested in small talk he replies 'Can I see your passport, ma'am?'

Believing it to be a formality, I confidently hand it to him.

'Where is your entry permit?' he continues.

'What entry permit?' I ask. Already I sense that those three Immigration goons have failed to do their job and I am in trouble.

'When you entered the country you would have been given an entry permit.'

'Well, I was given nothing. Three Immigration Officers looked at my passport. They did ask dozens of questions but they were all about my journey through Mexico. I told them that I had been anticipating difficulties arriving on a bike without any airline tickets, but they assured me all was well. I have to say that I felt surprised at the time.'

He is unconvinced and confiscates my passport. (This is not the time to re-enact my third tug of war over this document. This man is not to be messed with. His attitude towards me would not be out of place if dealing with a gang of armed, drug smuggling, illegal immigrants.)

'Proceed directly to the building and wait for me.' He returns to his patrol vehicle and telephones his colleagues. (With news of his big catch of the day?)

I am led into a large room with a long table in the middle. Chained to the floor along one side of this table are ten chairs and in front of each chair a pair of handcuffs is secured to the table.

'Sit down' he commands. There is no offer of coffee and cookies.

'You say you came over a bridge from Mexico. Which bridge was that?'

'It was the one which crosses over at Brownsville.'

'There are lots of bridges. What was it called?'

'I've no idea what it was called. There were road signs for several miles leading into Matamoros indicating *'Puente International'*. More than that I can't tell you.'

'They are all international bridges. What was this one called?'

'I really can't tell you any more than that. I found a bridge leading over into the States and crossed it. It only took five minutes to cycle from there to the Chamber of Commerce if that helps identify it.'

'How many officers checked you on arrival?'

At least I knew the answer to this one. 'Three – all men. There was a woman in the kiosk at the end of the bridge who had pointed me in their direction.'

'What colour were their uniforms?'

There is a strong temptation to yell *'Who the hell cares? What's going on here? Do I look like a drug dealer? How could I possibly be carrying any drugs when there isn't even room in my luggage for a hairbrush?'*

Instead I say meekly 'To be honest I wasn't paying that much attention, nor am I the world's most observant person. But I think that they were grey.'

As he continues with an aggressive line of questioning where even my birthplace of South Africa is sneered at and appears to be a disadvantage, I point out that my arrival had hardly been low profile. I had mistakenly set off a rape alarm in the presence of these three officers and had spent most of the morning being interviewed by the local media. I dare even to suggest that a couple of phone calls would quickly establish these facts.

During the two hours that I am held he searched through various books and files. Was he trying to find one which covered *'lone menopausal female cyclist'*? He made several phone calls during which I could hear the words 'She says....' again and again, as if I had been inspired to fabricate the whole story. He also spent a significant amount of time with one of his colleagues in an office and I could see them both through the glass in animated discussion while they glanced continuously at me.

My captor eventually, and with extreme reluctance, allows me to leave.

'Well, I guess I'll have to let you go.'

What an eighteen carat jerk. However bored he might have been, harassment was surely not a legitimate cure.

There is no need to phone Justin but it felt like a close call.

Chapter Twenty-Two

Moving on each day and making random choices about which door to approach, it is inevitable that no two receptions will be the same. The second night is a huge contrast, not least of all because it is the first house I approach which gets a positive result. A couple are outside working on a porch and immediately encourage me to make myself at home. They set out a chair on the lawn, tell me to help myself to iced drinks and insist the shampoo, soap and towels are all at my disposal when I take a shower. (The final proof that you have arrived in the US of A is when you turn on the shower and end up pinned against the opposite wall from the jet propelled force of water.)

As darkness falls they invite me to join them for supper where the pudding is a huge home made chocolate brownie and we all end up sitting on the porch chatting. When I return to the tent they are adamant that I *'holla'* if there's a problem during the night. In the morning I am not allowed to leave before joining the family for a huge breakfast. All is indeed well in my world.

At the end of a particularly gruelling one hundred mile ride I hit the jackpot at the first attempt. Ignoring such signs as *'Trespassers Will Be Shot'* and *'Beware Of Dangerous Guard Dogs'*, I struggle wearily up a long steep drive towards a lovely single story farmhouse where a man in his early twenties is doing some noisy welding. In spite of the dogs insistent barking, it takes several minutes before Dan notices me. Without hesitation he points to a grassy paddock, a fridge full of iced beers and a self contained furnished bungalow with an invitation to help myself to anything I might need. In spite of the temptation of the bungalow, I opt for the tranquillity of the paddock and the unimaginable thrill during the warm evening of lying on the grass and gazing up at the stars through the latticework of branches.

Before he returns to the farmhouse Dan says 'Oh by the way, there is a high security prison a mile or so from here. It was only a few months ago that they had a break out and one of the convicts happened to stumble over in this direction. He ended up crossing my land. So if you do hear any noise in the night, be sure to come and fetch me.'

'That's OK' I reply, not feeling too concerned. 'Perhaps I'll point him in the direction of the beers in the refrigerator and try and convince him that my bike would not make an ideal escape vehicle.'

Breakfast continues to be my favourite meal and where better than the full American version. With the abundant presence of diners, it is easy to avoid McDonalds and other fast junk outlets. Often either the owner or customers would make the connection with me and the bicycle, always propped outside in view. This would lead to many conversations while eating the biscuits (scones in English), hash browns and easy over eggs, and frequently I would not be allowed to pay for my meal. As so often since leaving I come to realise how inadequate *'thank you'* is .

But McDonalds does play a vital role on many days. Tipped off by John, my generous host for a few days in San Antonio, I push to the limit the offer of senior coffee with free refills – weak perhaps, but only 27 cents. Sometimes it fulfils the perfect way to spend half an hour recovering strength in my legs and sensation in my bum. On one occasion, having been caught in a downpour, the hot air hand drier in the ladies is used with great effect to blow dry all my clothes. The restroom also proves the perfect place to clean off all the grease after fixing a puncture, which Alchemy thoughtfully has right under the golden arches.

After a vicious day battling against horizontal rain and a vile head wind on a busy commuter highway, I turn off randomly into a residential side road. Plenty of houses to choose from –

plenty of potential or inventive rejections lurking behind each door. After a mile or so of glancing from side to side, it is a quirky blue house which attracts attention for the first attempt. Something to do with the roses in the garden, perhaps. Soaked and dreading a long search I take a deep breath and knock. The door is opened by a fifty-something hippy wearing boxer shorts, a bandana and earrings, and holding his grandson in his arms. The day and my sense of humour are salvaged.

'That is indeed an usual request' Rick says, echoing my words. 'And by the way, I must ask – are you a mass murderer?'

'All that I could murder right now is a hot drink' I tell him.

'Well, that's OK, but I must remind you that you are in Texas and if you do anything to upset me I shall have to shoot you. Come right on in.'

Within minutes Rick has produced a steaming bowl of vegetable soup and is telling me his life story. It is three days later that I set off on the road to Galveston having been treated as a royal visitor.

As the campsites in the States are several hundred miles apart it is unlikely that I will have the chance to use very many. The one in Galveston is isolated fifteen miles west of the town – more than an hour's ride to the nearest restaurants or shops (very bad news for a hungry cyclist at the end of a day's ride). Equally irritating – the cost is $15, whether for a mile long caravan or a four foot bicycle. The word caravan translates in to 'RV' – a recreational vehicle representing every modern luxury on wheels and so big that it is capable of towing a four wheel drive behind, dwarfed in comparison, as well as two motorbikes strapped to the front. This RV gets hooked up to electricity allowing use of: air conditioning, heating, lights, hot water, television, radio, cooker, microwave, kettle, food mixer, coffee percolator, computer, hair dryer, charger for mobile phone and other such essential camping equipment. This connection to electricity is of no value to a cyclist so I attempt to get my money's worth from the shower.

It is in Galveston that the first opportunity arises to follow Frank's advice about sending emails from the States. Because home ownership of personal computers is very high, internet cafés are rarer than comfortable leather saddles – I never found one. In the States public libraries offer a free service to members so the critical question is will a non-local, alien in fact, be allowed access? Will my accent be my downfall instead of always working in my favour? I am greeted with civility and directions to the banks of computers where I log in with the usual thrill of anticipation. Receiving news from home never fails to be exciting and the internet makes it so amazingly easy. There is also plenty of time to settle down to replying. This approach never fails on the many occasions that I use the public libraries all the way to the East coast.

Since my journey started, I have been composing regular email messages. These have been sent to my indefatigable anchor, Diana, who has been forwarding them on to family, friends and (I gather) an ever-increasing number of interested parties. Each message has endeavoured to collate all the unfolding experiences of the ride, trying to capture the essence of how privileged I feel, as well as the agony, ecstasy, hunger, thirst, elation, exhaustion, relief, delight, astonishment, and above all the never-ending feeling of extraordinary synchronicity and good fortune. (Never again will I use the word coincidence.) I am constantly astonished how, at the press of a button, dozens of people all over the world will be aware of just what has been going on in my life. And the resultant pay-off is anticipating the thrill of receiving incoming mail with stories from home.

To travel east from Galveston, it is necessary to catch a ferry and another passenger, a chap who is on a motor bike, approaches me, curious about the panniers. During this short crossing, John learns my destination for the night, Winnie (coincidentally his home town) and also my tactics for finding a place to sleep. It crosses my mind to suggest that he could save me the bother if he has some spare lawn, but I chicken out and we disembark, heading to the same place but at significantly different speeds. Several hours later it is with surprise and delight that I see John riding towards me on his motorbike. He has calculated that The Team should be a couple of miles outside the town and has returned to offer me accommodation in his trailer. He doesn't need to twist my arm. By the time I arrive he has made fresh coffee, as well as the bed in his spare room. A divorced man in his forties, he treats me to a chicken sandwich for supper (collected in the car from a drive thru) and a huge breakfast at the Waffle House; he also insists on doing all my washing and gives me everything I need to take a shower.

'Consider it a blessing' he says. 'I'm the good guy.'

I pay a small price of having to listen to him singing as he accompanies himself on a guitar. No wasted talent here.

From start to finish of this journey I cross paths with seven other touring cyclists, all men and all very skinny. After Daniel, the second was a young Japanese staying in the hotel in Calcutta before cycling north to Nepal. Prior to leaving Japan he held down two jobs for three years while living with his parents in order to save money for his adventure. He had been on the road for two years and was vague about his destination. His English was being picked up en route and he told me with a beaming smile 'I am very happy. I am so very very happy.'

Another was Julian from Wales. I met him at the campsite in Galveston and apart from sharing grievances about the cost of pitching a tent, he told me that he had been held up at knife point in Guatemala and pulled the *'car boot sale wallet'* trick. (The idea is to buy a cheap old wallet, fill it with sheets of newspaper which are then wrapped up with a few dollars and hope that the muggers won't notice until much later.) He was approaching the end of his two and a half year journey during which he had to lay up for seven weeks due to illness and also had painful problems with his knees.

It was on the road from the ferry I encountered a very grumpy old German who had been on the road for seven years. I pulled up to say hello. In less than five minutes it became clear that he hated America because he had had so many negative experiences. I couldn't imagine how that could possibly be, but as he elaborated it became clear. He was choosing to camp rough, usually involving trespassing on private land. This resulted in being sworn at, if he was lucky, but more often shot at. (Guns are an essential part of everybody's life, it seems.) He refused to accept and conform to cultural standards, one of which is that it is not done to take a pee by the side of the road. Because of his own stupidity and ignorance he was constantly getting people's backs up and had been on the receiving end of many offensive comments to which he doubtless retaliated. It was impossible to feel any sympathy.

Chapter Twenty-Three

After just one day's cycling in America, it became clear that the only relevant question each morning was – what is the wind up to? Because all roads are straight, straight, straight, if you start the day with a hefty wind in your face, you know there's a battle ahead. Struggling against a strong head wind for hours, mile after mile, cold or hot, wet or dry, proved the only aspect of a day's ride that upset me. I discover that I am capable of a temper tantrum that a two year old would be proud of.

On leaving Winnie it is such a day. It takes almost four hours to struggle barely thirty miles (no hills slowing progress – just that vile wind) and there are no scenic diversions to ease the pain. A busy by-pass around Port Arthur is making it difficult to find anywhere just to pull off to eat the much longed for and by now urgently needed picnic. I spot a huge modern church with its own vast car park and turn in. A young Indian man emerges to find me sheltering in the lee of the building and amazingly doesn't flinch at the sight of a vagrant on the church doorstep. He is the vicar!

'I hope you don't mind' I explain 'but I've had an exhausting morning's ride and urgently needed to find somewhere to stop and have some lunch. I had been looking out for the last few miles but couldn't see anything remotely suitable. You can't imagine what a relief it is to have some shelter from that wind.'

'Why don't you come inside? I'm about to make myself a hot chocolate. It sounds as if you could do with one.' If I do have a god looking after me, this is as close as he's got and it's heavenly intervention of the most welcome kind.

I don't need any arm twisting and follow Stephen through the maze of rooms to the kitchen and then on to his office – this is like no church in England. After hearing my story, he offers the use of his laptop to check my emails and with rain now travelling horizontally across the window, suggests that I call it a day and stay in the fully furnished two bedroom house facing on to the other side of the car park.

'Are you absolutely sure?'

'Why, of course. It's only there for people like you' he replies convincingly.

With imperceptible hesitation and a dollop of guilt, I accept. The self promised target of fifty miles could be ignored – the morning's ride had felt like five hundred and fifty, so what the hell. After more shower therapy I relax in warm and comfortable surroundings, feeling incredibly fortunate. This is more proof of the abundance of synchronicity.

It is the night of the Presidential election and with two televisions in the living room it seems that an ideal way of spending the evening would be to tune in and check on how it is shaping up. But no, all channels are locked in to the god slots, so perhaps somewhat ungratefully I opt for the radio which is next to the bed. I realise next morning that having crashed out early I have not only missed out on the drama of the close and yet to be resolved result, I have regrettably missed an evening visitor. The evidence is on the doorstep – a magnificent selection of three home made salads, plus croutons, sour cream dip and a welcoming note. The food is enough to keep me going for three days.

This spontaneous gesture of Christian hospitality is not reflected on two other occasions during my time in America. In both instances my search amongst the private homes had proved unfruitful and the clock was ticking.

'Why don't you try the church?' came the advice from a woman anxious to get rid of me.

Churches come in many denominations, the buildings are very modern, very large and very well appointed – more a complex than a place of worship, reaching into the community in diverse ways. There are rooms for meetings, lectures, offices, catering facilities, rest rooms, huge car parks and even more space allocated to manicured gardens. Without a second thought I sought out the home of the Catholic vicar but a notice pinned above the letter box was not encouraging. It read 'Office (note that word 'Office') closed – St Somebody's day'. Undeterred, I knocked on the door to be greeted by an even less encouraging grim face and 'Yes?'

Hugely apologetic, I stated my case, as always with Alchemy by my side.

His excuses tumbled out and included: 'The team are playing football now' (yes the church had its own pitch); 'We have a children's lesson this evening'; 'There is a service later on'; 'People would be very concerned if they saw a tent'. But his body language indicated that he was struggling, knowing that fundamentally no Christian would turn away someone with such a simple request as a patch of grass for the night. Finally and very grudgingly he relented, pointing me in the direction of one of the several acres of church lawn. He then slammed the door and that was it. No food, no drink, no use of the bathroom, no fresh water. What was so infuriating next morning, with The Team all packed up about to leave, one of his parishioners called on him. This chap then approached me, intrigued by my story and wanting to know more, while the hypocritical vicar stood there bathing in undeserved glory – he claimed to have been my host for the night. I would bet he even found a way to incorporate it in his sermon. Something about a Good Samaritan perhaps....

The second 'when all else fails make the local vicar squirm' occasion comes about after a particularly demoralising and unproductive hour of variations on the 'not in my back yard' theme.

'Go to the church and ask for the vicar. Tell him that Doug sent you.' Doug is standing at his front door keen to pass the buck.

'OK, I'll do that.' Then, as a precaution I ask 'What's his name?

'Mr Jardine' replies Doug.

I cycle to the vicar's house and am knocking on the front door when he drives up. He is unmistakably livid to find a vagrant on his doorstep. His car window flies open and he demands to know what my purpose is.

'What are you doing here? What is it that you want?' in the sort of tone that makes me want either to retreat in terror or give him a good slapping.

But I do neither. I don't even answer the question. Instead I ask 'Are you Mr Jardine?' This completely floors him. He is visibly stunned and taken aback and would undoubtedly prefer to deny it – anything to get rid of me. Instant conversion to an agnostic perhaps.

'I am looking for somewhere to pitch my tent for the night. Doug suggested that you might be able to help.'

Doug is in danger of excommunication. Having posed the simple question, I know instinctively it's now best to remain silent and let him sweat in his huge air conditioned car.

And anyway, why should I let him off the hook? *'Oh, sorry to have been such a nuisance and so demanding. Don't you worry about me, vicar. You just go into your comfortable home. I promise not to mess up two square yards of your church land. I'll just find a comfortable pavement and hope that by the time the morning arrives I haven't been mugged, raped or murdered. Please, no, I would hate to trouble your sanctimonious existence.'*

What follows is very much an action replay of the previous vicar encounter, only this one is a Methodist, married with two children. He sits squirming in the car saying *'no'* in every possible way; excuses about upsetting the locals, my own personal danger, inconvenience for parishioners, nowhere to pitch the tent, arousing suspicion of police. But as long as I stand my ground the outcome is inevitable – he will have to relent which he does, with incredibly bad grace. Does this man practise what he preaches? Has he even heard of the Good Samaritan? He demands to see my passport which he takes to the church office to photocopy and insists on confirmation of precisely what time I will be leaving tomorrow morning. He directs me to the children's playground (yes, that's right – fully furnished with everything children under the age of ten could possibly want and part of the church facilities). I am surprised not to be ordered to restore the flattened patch of grass with a brush before leaving, but not surprised that that is the last I see of him.

I am only too aware that my major doorstep selling point is that I am self contained and won't need to intrude in any way – and this is effectively true – but it has to be worth noting that the only two occasions during my journey through the southern States of America where the level of hospitality was a big fat zilch were in the presence of incumbents of the church. Not so much as a glass of water or use of the rest room.

This might sound harsh, but it is important to emphasise that with the amount of land that belongs to these churches, to allow me to pitch the tent overnight was really no big deal, however much the vicar might not have wanted to allow me into his home. On the other hand it is extremely understandable that the private house owner might well be inclined to deny my request. Their refusals shed an entirely new light on the *'not in my back yard'* category of excuses. They also demonstrated just how fast and imaginatively people can think on their front doorstep.

Here is a selection:

'I will have to phone my brother to ask his permission and he is out of town for the next two days.'

'There is no-one in who lives here just now' (with four cars/pick-ups parked on the drive).

'My room mates are asleep – come back in a couple of hours.'

'My husband might be angry.'

'My husband would not be happy with that.'

'I'll have to ask my husband but that's not possible because he is at a meeting which won't be over for another hour.'

'I'd be happy to but them ol' red ants will eat ya orl up.'

'Try my neighbours.'

'Try the public park in the town.' (Illegal by the way – I did check this one out with the police.)

'Try the church.' (Yeah, right, good idea....)

'My husband is uncomfortable with visitors.'

'My lease doesn't allow anyone to camp in the yard.'

'I'm leasing the property and about to move out.'

'My cousins are expected this evening.'

'I have to get written permission if anyone other than the family stays over.'

'We're out for the evening.' (With no room for shampoo would the family heirlooms be in danger?)

'I'm not comfortable with that idea.'

And indeed, why should they tolerate the intrusion of a total stranger? These excuses were entirely reasonable and I was never about to stand there and argue my case.

It is in Bishop that I hit the jackpot of dismissal. It is one of three teenagers who opens the door, invites me inside, offers me an iced drink and then phones his father and step mother to let them know that they have an unexpected visitor. When the step mother refuses to believe him, he passes the phone to me to prove he isn't hallucinating on an illegal substance. Her voice is colder than the ice in my water and the father immediately comes on the line.

'I am intending to cut my lawn this evening and after that I plan to spread fertiliser on the grass.' He then adds 'You've probably noticed how long it is' (Well, no actually – other priorities on my mind.) 'My neighbours will be worth a try.'

Wise to this one I ask 'OK, that's great. I quite understand. Could you please tell me which side they live and also their name?'

'Oh, well, ummm ahhh I didn't mean anybody in particular. Just someone else along the street might be able to help.' With that he hangs up.

The son is intrigued by my story and we are chatting when his father phones back to check if I am still here. The poor lad is given instructions to chuck me out.

'My father and stepmother are returning home with company and then they are all going to watch the local football.' (Would that be before or after cutting and fertilising the grass? Or perhaps in between. Perhaps the *'company'* will cut while he fertilises so that they will get to the game on time. The fact that the whole lawn is covered in Halloween decorations could possibly slow them up a bit. Either way, this man is definitely in for a hectic evening.) The son is utterly mortified.

'This should never have happened. They are just making excuses. I am so embarrassed but I can only apologise. Had it been up to me, you could willingly have stayed in my room. You wouldn't even have needed your tent. And, by the way, don't bother asking anybody else in this street. They are all as ignorant as my parents.'

Strong words from the young man who shook my hand warmly as I left.

Chapter Twenty-Four

Detours are never welcome and even more irksome when deemed entirely unnecessary which is the case on the approach into the town of Lake Charles. The only access from the west is over a bridge, which turns out to be a bridge denied rather than a bridge too far. Crossing water in whatever form always gives me a thrill, whether by ferry or bridge. Ferries are relaxing, the only effort required is to watch one shore diminish as the other looms larger. Apart from the one over the English Channel, ferries have ranged from very small to tiny, the most quaint of which was across the Danube. Built to carry just a few bicycles, it operates by pulling on a chain attached to both shores – the strength of the current would have made anything else expensive or impossible. The ferries in Vietnam cost but a few pence and were packed with cyclists and pedestrians.

As for the bridges.... The two noteworthy ones in Europe, over the Moselle and the Rhine, were barely recognisable as a bridge, indistinguishable from the road on either side, such was the seamless transition. This did not detract from the excitement and sense of progress at the time. Pakistan and India provided four significant bridges, sadly over virtually dry river beds. Each bridge was several hundred yards long and every four yards there was an inexplicable and worrying gaping chasm across the width of the bridge – anything up to eight inches wide – which made for uncomfortable cycling. It was on one of these bridges in Pakistan that I came across a dozen workmen, squatting on the curb, each with a dustpan and brush, sweeping out the gutter.

In the States the bridges take on a very different design, forming a huge arc reaching towards the sky and by definition, the wider the crossing the higher the arc. They can be so impressive that from the saddle of a bicycle it appears as if you are at the foot of a ski jump and because the other side drops away, they look for all intents and purposes as if they stop in mid-air.

It is such a bridge which leads into Lake Charles, bigger by far than its predecessors and displaying a sign *'Cyclists and Pedestrians Prohibited'*. My temptation to ignore this is tempered by my fear of being hauled up by the police, which is what brings about the twenty mile detour.

This delays my arrival at Iowe, the planned destination and with daylight vanishing and a wicked storm imminent, it seems prudent to embark on the door knocking routine some miles before the town. The only problem is that houses are very spread out each with a long drive and it takes considerable time to get to the front door, just to find nobody home. Perhaps it's advisable to carry on the extra few miles. But no, it's jackpot time again. The first door is opened by Betty, who is holding her young grandson and wearing a huge smile; her husband is behind with an even bigger smile. There is no hint of that *'yes – what do you want?'* expression, or worse by far a friendly *'howdy – what can I do to help?'* followed by a reply that boils down to *'well, I didn't really mean it'*.

On hearing my well rehearsed request she says 'This is absolutely wonderful – the last time we had a cyclist knock on our door he stayed with us for a week'.

With the sky now black they would not hear of my putting up the tent, leading me instead to a beautiful guest room and seconds later the storm erupts dumping enough water during the next two hours to have tested my swimming skills and floated the tent away. As often happened, members of the family are phoned with the news that a woman has turned up on a bike from England and many of them drive over throughout the evening to learn more. Also as often happened, Betty invites me to stay for a week but I resist the temptation and set off next day, grateful to accept a bag of satsumas picked that morning and a couple of drops of WD40 on the remaining lock which has become stiff and difficult to open.

(Earlier that day the other one had to be binned. Alchemy had been secured to railings while I bought my food and nothing I could do would persuade the key to turn. It was jammed solid and a handy man from the supermarket saved the day by sawing through the plastic covered chain. I certainly couldn't risk this happening again.)

A peaceful day's ride brings a peaceful end to the following day. Spotting a rare sight, a person leaving her car and entering her home, this door is the obvious choice for my knock. The lady turns out to be Ruby, a sprightly eighty five year old. She was borne in this house but it is the garden which is exceptional as it consists almost entirely of flower beds – a mass of colour for all seasons. She used to own a florist shop and her green fingers had produced a lifetime's reward. There is just about enough lawn to pitch the tent and she insists that I join her for supper and breakfast, with the added bonus of freshly squeezed orange juice. She even leaves the back door open so that I have access to her downstairs bathroom throughout the night. Quite remarkably gutsy at her age. She is horrified to think that I might miss all the sightseeing delights ahead and gives me chapter and verse on to where to go and what to see.

As a result of her enthusiasm, I decide to take a voluntary detour to check out the home of Tabasco Sauce – that familiar bottle on the shelf of every kitchen throughout the world. It comes as a real shock to find a tiny factory hidden away on an island at the end of a twelve mile stretch of road leading nowhere. Buried in the swamps of Louisiana, it is difficult to imagine just how this peppery product has gathered such international recognition. The four hours out of my day is only just worth it because it is Friday – the day when the factory is closed – so it is not possible to watch production, the only real incentive for my visit. Settling for watching a short video on a small screen doesn't bring the same buzz of satisfaction and I can't even supplement my lunch with the freebie snacks as the pepper sauce has always been way too hot for my taste.

Louisiana is the land of black magic and white witches and Ellie, my woolly companion, is still tied prominently on Alchemy's handlebars and without the benefit of daily showers, she is looking decidedly grubby and travel weary. However, in spite of the dust, her hair is still very black and plentiful and she is the perfect incarnation of a Voodoo doll. There have been some strong reactions on doorsteps at the sight of her – who would have imagined that gesture of kindness way back in Hungary could have cost a night's accommodation? Whatever impressions people might have of me, I never expected to be taken as a witch.

With the banks of the Mississippi in my sights, my search for that patch of grass is going badly. My antennae are always tuned in for activity in or around the houses and I notice the reversing lights of a car and decide to knock on the driver's window. Approaching anybody about to leave home cannot be deemed sensible, but prompted by darkening sky, falling temperatures and an hour's worth of rejections, I choose to ignore any instincts about bad timing.

Far from the dismissal I am braced for, the driver says 'Yes, make yourself at home. We're off to church'. 'Home' means the garden and when he and his wife return the tent is set up for the night and the swing chair has being put to good use writing up the day's notes. The couple vanish into the house with barely a word and it seems that is it for the night. But no, having changed into jeans, Myles re-appears – to suss me out. After a short time he invites me in and my tent spends a frosty night on its own. The flood gates of hospitality open, including access to my emails. In the morning The Team is loaded into the back of the pick-up because Myles and Linda are keen to show me one of the local homesteads, a plantation which has been featured several times in films and documentaries. We then drive along the Mississippi levy and I am dropped off the other side of the bridge on the road to New Orleans. Myles had phoned the State troopers to check whether or not bicycles were allowed to cross this one and they did not know. Neither did the local traffic police.

It has become clear by now that I could have done almost the entire journey from Texas to the East Coast in a pick-up truck. Nearly every home that I stayed in had one and without fail the man would offer to transport me the next sixty miles, one hundred even, down the road. For a nation who walks less than two miles a month – to and from the shopping mall car park – it is inconceivable that anyone would choose to ride when there is a comfortable, air-conditioned alternative. Is it possible that evolution will replace people's legs with wheels similar to those castors on office chairs?

(One evening the tent had been set up in a private wood but I was invited into the house for coffee during the evening. The woman was so overweight that she used such a chair to move around her home.)

A few days earlier careful thought had to be given about visiting New Orleans. This was prompted by absolutely everyone – men and women – warning about the real dangers lurking in its streets. It is reputed to be the most dangerous city in America. For me it represented a major highlight, one which I was so much looking forward to. Anyway, The Team has travelled safely through countries which many considered too dangerous. Would it really be necessary to bypass a city for this reason? The answer had to be no.

On arrival I book into a hostel and decide to stay for three days. Some of this time is occupied by going on tours or eating freshly baked French doughnuts, but the highlights are cruising around on Alchemy, either in the French Quarter or amongst beautiful houses in the residential areas. (I am the victim of a theft – someone has taken all my picnic provisions from the hostel fridge!)

I cycle out of New Orleans in rain more suitable to the Indian monsoon season. My waterproof top was proving anything but, so in an effort to remain at least partially dry I have adapted a black bin liner to do the job. Hardly a fashion statement but remarkably effective.

Around midday and very much in the middle of nowhere, I am delighted to see a boatyard teeming with activity as this gives me a chance to check just where I am. All eyebrows are raised as this dripping plastic bag walks in. Peeling the sopping mittens off frozen fingers, I produce the map and ask the assembled gathering to confirm how far I have come. I am fervently hoping that there will not be much further to go. Pitching the tent in the rain and climbing into it soaking wet seems preferable to many more miles of cycling misery.

Having refreshed the parts that only hot coffee can reach (the chap serving would not hear of me paying for it), I splash back to Alchemy and am deciding whether wearing the soggy mittens will serve any purpose, when a chap who had been drinking beer amongst the group follows me out and offers me a lift – my destination is ten miles away. So why not? Without any dedication or commitment to cycle every inch of this journey, the dry, warm, if somewhat dilapidated van seems a preferable alternative. Anticipating a ten mile ride, I choose to ignore the fact that he drinks one more beer before we leave and drives off clutching another.

He is going to visit his brother Ben in Biloxi, fifty miles along the coast and on my planned route for the following day. With the rain intensifying and temperatures plummeting, it is very easy to resist getting out after the ten miles.

In spite of Remi's description of his brother as 'the Jew with fishhooks in his pockets', Ben is generous and hospitable, taking both of us out to dinner and suggesting that it would be sensible for me to stay until the storm passes – which could be two or three days. An unexpected bonus is that he is a professional musician and we listen to him accompanying jazz tapes on his flugelhorn – so much more rewarding than the rowdiness and drunkenness of the bars in New Orleans. However, Remi does his best to recreate both, definitely a man who likes his beer which prompts him to prattle on and on more than is necessary or welcome.

Remi has a different slant on his brother's offer.

'He doesn't really mean it. He's just being a gentleman. I know that he would prefer to go to New Orleans for the weekend. His friends are going to be there and he wants to meet up with them. They'll be playing at one of the bars. If you stay, this means that he'll miss out and I'll never hear the end of it. I'll be blamed because I'm the one who brought you here. It'll be my fault that he was caught up and he'll never let me forget it. He'll be complaining for months to come.'

It is difficult to believe. Ben has gone to extensive lengths to make me feel welcome. He has pointed out where his food is kept, even putting the vegetarian bits and pieces on the worktop. He's indicated where all his books are and even trusted me with the television remote – the biggest complement by far, as this is the most important piece of equipment in any American home. A pretty convincing act for someone who apparently does not want me around.

Although it isn't yet seven o'clock in the morning, Ben has disappeared and Remi is about to leave. The choices are: to ride out the storm by not riding Alchemy and remain in the comfort and dry of Ben's trailer. (When do the words 'Bye for now, Pam. Be sure to make yourself at home and I'll look forward to seeing you later' not mean what they say?); to continue along the coast with the Remi in the van; or load up and pedal off with the guarantee of at least two days of rain bearing all the characteristics of a power shower without the hot water.

This is what being between a rock and a hard place must feel like. The last thing I want is more of Remi's company. But to set off on Alchemy in the horizontal and freezing rain would be worse than either the rock or the hard place. My gut feeling tells me that Ben's offer was genuine, but maybe not.... I also have a strong suspicion that Remi is lonely and wants company. Insanely, I ignore my instinct and climb aboard.

His plan is to get to Pensacola, fifty miles away but the van has other ideas; it is allergic to the rain. The entire day is spent swapping a spluttering, reluctant and decrepit van for a Mercedes saloon which is parked up to its axles in mud in a caravan park and has a flat battery and two flat tyres. The only comforting and recurring thoughts are *'What else would I be doing?'* plus the fact that Remi is functioning on caffeine rather than alcohol and has become very silent and morose. I resign myself to the role of *'interested and sure glad I'm single'* spectator. If my friends could see me now.... By the time we reach Pensacola it is eight o'clock and Remi is intent on a pitcher of beer.

He is keen to introduce me to his favourite drinking holes, the first of which is an *'Irish pub'* and I am not surprised to find that there is nothing either pub or Irish about the place. Its trademark is to pin dollar bills to the ceiling and walls, together with brassieres and other unbankable underwear. Remi then sets about doing what he does best – drinking pitchers of beer. (I calculated that the jug holds four to five pints.) If one goes along with the theory regarding the consuming of alcohol which is: one is sufficient; two is too many; and three's not enough, then Remi definitely belongs to the *'three's not enough'* category. Not nearly enough....

Any idea of escape has to be discarded until the morning. Not only is it dark, cold and still raining hard, but all my gear is jammed tight in the back seat of his Mercedes amongst the clutter of his welding tools and several boxes, so disentangling it is not something I can do on my own.

Two pitchers later (of which I drink one glass) we move to the second haunt, this time Mexican. His enthusiasm, joy and familiarity on meeting the woman who owns the establishment is not reciprocated. He reminisces about his singing on previous visits and it is evident that her opinion of the success and popularity of the occasions conjure up very different images. I am beginning to feel incredibly uneasy about the situation but it is too late. Two more pitchers of beer are dispatched down his throat and he becomes loud and incoherent, approaching everyone as if they are his best friend. He upsets both the bouncers on the door and the staff behind the bar are disgusted with him. His plan had been for us to stay the night with an ex-girlfriend but this option disappeared along with the beer. My only choice is to demand the car keys and seek peace in the front seat of his car.

This has without a shadow of doubt been the worst twenty four hours since leaving home.

One thing is certain – no matter what the weather, the morning will see me back on my bicycle. One can have too much of a good thing. To be in control of my life is more important than personal warmth or comfort.

With the cotton fields now behind, I am in Florida and it is Sunday morning when I arrive in De Funiak Springs, a town where it is possible I might have a contact. (The prospect of not having to go through the random knocking routine is surprisingly uplifting, perhaps an indication of the depth of anxiety attached to the daily procedure.) But the only way to confirm this is to access my emails and the quaint and tiny library is shut. Believing that someone with local knowledge might be able to suggest another option, I am wondering what to do because all the shops are closed and pedestrians are not just an endangered species, they are as extinct as the dinosaur. So, where to go, who to ask? Another perfect moment of synchronicity. The congregation of a quaint and tiny church opposite are coming down the steps, each man and woman stopping to shake hands with the vicar. I take my chance and cross over.

'Good morning. I'm sorry to bother you but I'm trying to find somewhere that I can log on to the Internet. I'm expecting a message from my brother and am very keen to read my emails.'

The congregation is elderly and to the majority (amongst whom I feel like a mere spring chicken) I might have been speaking a foreign language. The message is passed around and nobody has a clue what I'm talking about but far from dismissive, they suggest that I join them for their Thanksgiving lunch while a solution is found. Fantasies are based on what happens next, especially if you have lost two stone in weight and are permanently hungry. There is a feast of home made food laid out in the community room behind the vicarage and all that is asked of me is to contain my drooling long enough to check my messages. The vicar has a computer with an Internet connection – the electronic route to his god perhaps – and a subsequent phone call establishes contact with my prospective hosts. The banquet reflects the pride and skill with which it has been made. By the time I leave there are several alternative offers of hospitality should the original one fall through.

Snow is falling when I knock on Liz and Dave's door.

The Thanksgiving weekend is a significant family occasion in the American calendar. I have been feeling apprehensive about my vagabond status during this national holiday as any intrusion could be viewed as bad timing – even vicars could be forgiven for turning me away. But thanks to Dave and Liz the problem evaporates. Thanksgiving is next weekend and they have persuaded me to stay – phenomenal generosity from total strangers who were contacted by my brother via an internet site. Their offer comes across as so genuine that even token resistance seems ridiculous, with the result that together with their cat, Liz's mother and a couple of single male friends, we enjoy yet more food. The traditional fare is turkey and stuffing together with numerous vegetables and salads, followed by pumpkin pie and apple pie for dessert. As with Christmas, the major pay off for all this work is the left-overs which are enjoyed for days to come.

On leaving I try inadequately to thank Dave and Liz for their kindness and wish them happy, healthy and peaceful days to come. To my horror Dave replies 'Back on you, babe'. Until now I believed that *'Missing you already'* was as bad as it could get.

Chapter Twenty Five

The journey north continues with frosty mornings under clear blue skies. On leaving the coastal area the flat terrain becomes significantly hilly – quite a shock to my poor legs which have been having an easy time for a while, particularly as the average daily mileage is still around eighty.

Back on the road my luck continues to hold – it is the first house which brings success. After an unpromising start where a woman in a dressing gown tells me to wait while she asks her husband (often an excuse to get rid of me), they both re-appear and a ten minute doorstep consultation takes place. This dispels any doubts about how genuine I am, so Tracey and James invite me in and I demolish more of those delicious left-overs. They then call in a local newspaper journalist to interview me, after which they drive a sixty mile round trip to show me Christmas City – a drive thru Christmas lights show. The night is spent in the privacy, warmth and comfort of their pool (as in swimming) room with mattress, bedding, electric blanket and heater (all of which Tracey carried out from the house). She was keen to save me the hassle of unpacking the camping gear.

I join them for breakfast but am concerned that this might lead to accompanying them to the church service, as much of the yesterday evening's conversation was about religion.

They also elaborated their feelings on 'We've got no problems with coloured people, but…. ' It is this 'but' that was so scary because it reflected so many conversations with so many families throughout my time in America and the 'but' went on for hours.

Tracey and James demonstrated this prejudice by saying how they had driven miles further than they wanted to find a motel which was not owned by Indians (who have moved very successfully into this area of business.) They also own several guns and would not hesitate to use them if the occasion arose.

And they go to church every Sunday. Fortunately they are not expecting me to join them and as always I am genuinely thrilled to have experienced their spontaneous generosity and kindness.

They stand at the gate waving and say 'Thank you for choosing our house.'

I discover that the concept of Drive Thru is pushed to the limit as it does not stop at fast food and viewing Christmas lights. It extends to banking, video shops and pawnbrokers. Most bizarre was the *'Walk-In Divorce and Bankruptcy'* (in the same building!) And there were the most appalling of corny names: *'Blinds Of All Kinds'; 'Seeds And Feeds'; 'Bookays 4U'; 'State Of The Art For The Heart'; 'Kuntry Kusins'; 'Slug A Bug Inc'; 'John's Alibi'* (what could that be about?)

How different is the following evening. After several hills too far, I am forced to the limit of endurance and daylight because that night's destination turns out to be merely a name on the map – no houses, not even a church – and it is now gone four o'clock. Forced to continue towards Lumpkin, I am relieved to find a few houses scattered on the outskirts of the town. With the sun plummeting towards the horizon, I spot a woman on her doorstep with three kids so I pedal up. (Somebody home – what a relief.) Her response is unique and at least as creative anything previously conjured up.

'My home is not set up with restrooms for visitors.'

'I assure you that is not a problem for me. If you wouldn't mind just letting me pitch my tent I can't tell you how grateful I would be. I've cycled over eighty miles and would really appreciate not having to go any further. I won't need to trouble you at all.'

'I'll have to ask my husband. Please wait.'

The husband appears and gives his permission with the caution 'Be careful where you put the tent. There are a couple of dead trees which could fall down on top of you. Also, avoid the area where the septic tank is.'

Squished or suffocated – a rare choice. With that the door is shut with no further comment. It is now dark and very cold so I waste no time in getting organised. Half an hour later this strange and timid woman re-appears with a tray of Thanksgiving left-overs and sits outside in the Arctic conditions to talk while I eat. Her role in life is to educate their son, a shy, withdrawn young teenager who had stared curiously at me when I arrived. His only companions are the two girls who live next door and are half his age. This was the group who were on the doorstep earlier. I am shocked to learn that the family don't own a computer and the father uses the only car to get to work. With the house several miles from the town and no local friends his own age, this young boy must lead a strange existence.

His mother tells me that the house is a mess, as a background to confirming that it would be alright to use the bathroom before going to bed. (When I took on the role of Avon Lady during the early years of my marriage, the given greeting from every woman of every age who opened the door was unfailingly *'I'm sorry the house is so untidy'*.) It is easy to assure her that every woman always perceives her house to be untidy. But no, it turns out that she has, if anything, understated the truth. No wonder her initial knee jerk reaction on seeing me was to protect herself from any intrusion. It is embarrassing. I have to pick my way through the debris piled high in the passage, passing open doors revealing rooms where the colour of the carpet cannot be detected for the junk on the floor. She goes ahead of me into the bathroom and spends a couple of minutes cleaning the toilet. When I return to the garden, she lends me a blanket to keep hypothermia at bay and I imagine has far exceeded her own expectations of offering hospitality. As always, I am extremely grateful.

A repeated and annoying scenario is when people refuse any idea of my tent on their grass but are happy to stand on their doorstep quizzing me about my journey. Their curiosity could waste half an hour, still leaving the unsolved problem of where I would be sleeping. My rule is: sorry chum – no patch of grass, no snippet of story. This particular evening I have approached a man sweeping fallen leaves. It is an ambivalent situation: is he the gardener or the owner? No means of telling, and worse still he is very curious and asks lots of questions – perhaps a welcome distraction from raking leaves. But without a definite *'no'* it feels premature to walk away and his manner is educated and charming.

Mike eventually volunteers 'Sue, my wife and I run our home as a bed and breakfast for tourists or visiting business men and women. It would be way out of order to have a tent pitched in the yard. We have three lawyers from Atlanta staying over tonight which would mean awkward questions.'

Assuming, wrongly, that a B&B is a cheaper option than a hotel I say 'Yes, I can understand that, so perhaps it's time to spoil myself. How much would I have to pay for the room for one night?'

On learning that the cost is $105 (without breakfast), the idea is instantly dispelled.

Somewhat half heartedly I suggest that the tent might be pitched out of the way so that the lawyers won't spot it. (Perhaps we could camouflage it to look like another pile of leaves.) But Mike is adamant. 'No, I'm sorry. That would be entirely inappropriate.'

Telling me to wait he disappears while I look at my watch.

He returns with Sue and says 'I've told her all about you and we both agree that we would be delighted to have you as our guest for the night. You will be welcome to have dinner with us this evening and breakfast before you leave but there are two conditions.'

I thought it all sounded too good to be true and stop breathing at this point.

'The first is, please don't mention the fact that we're not charging you anything to the lawyers. They don't need to know. And secondly, we would prefer it if you were gone by eight o'clock tomorrow morning.'

Whow – again, it doesn't get any better than this. Their home is superbly furnished with elegant antiques and luxurious fixtures and fittings. As for eight o'clock – this is a lie-in for me.

It turns out that there is no danger of my oversleeping because their sumptuous house is within yards of a level crossing. While passenger trains might be infrequent, freight trains more than compensate. They are several miles long and the regulations state they hoot and hoot and hoot again when approaching a level crossing. Until just recently every night's sleep had been interrupted by mosquitoes (blissfully no longer around thanks to the cold), but tonight it's the turn of the engine drivers. Throughout the entire night these trains just kept on coming.

There is a wonderful quote in Mike and Sue's brochure. It reads '…. having the opportunity to experience the sights and sounds of one of the oldest railroad crossings.' (Perhaps to avoid lawsuits from visiting lawyers.)

Atlanta, Georgia is the single unshiftable landmark of my journey because my brother, Justin, lives there with his family. All along the ambition has been to cycle unannounced up to his house, knock on the front door and ask if I could pitch my tent for the night. A genuine dream, but scuppered in a weak moment on the phone. I reach Fayetteville, a few miles south of the Atlanta ring road (a ten lane interstate, eighty miles in circumference and banned to bicycles). It is midday which does not leave enough time to tackle the journey to the north east area of the city where Justin lives. Very excited I can't resist phoning to say I'll be arriving tomorrow, which results in Betsy driving down to collect me. The perfect place to wait is a nearby restaurant cum bakery and treat myself to ultimate comfort food of foaming hot chocolate accompanied by a chocolate brownie. The owner, a German woman in her mid-thirties, is a keen cyclist and offers me a bed for the night. The opportunities are overwhelming, even when I'm not looking.

This reinforces the feeling that I have let myself down by allowing Betsy to collect me – my resistance was pathetic and very unconvincing – but from the safety of the passenger seat it is easy to understand why everybody from Texas onwards has commented on the traffic in Atlanta and how dangerous cycling would be. In fact, the real challenge would have been navigating the fifty miles through suburbia and the city centre. On balance I am very grateful for the lift and as if to prove the point sleep most of the following day.

It is amazing to discover just how easy it is to slip, indeed avalanche into being a total slob. I stay over until just after Christmas which we spend in Vero Beach, Florida, the intention being to continue the journey from there up the east coast and then head in to Charlotte to catch a flight home.

When we say goodbye it is cold, wet, windy, miserable and somehow pointless. I could return with the family to Atlanta and call it a day. But that doesn't feel right and my mind is made up. Justin and the family are visiting the Kennedy Space Centre for the day and Betsy has left the key to the house under the mat in case I have a change of mind. I really wish she hadn't.

Chapter Twenty Six

Just to get back into the swing of things it seems appropriate to stop especially early and cut out any last minute dramas about where I will be sleeping. The town of Titusville has other ideas as it offers up nothing but rejects. One petrified woman goes so far as to shut her garage door from inside by remote as I approach. Have I lost the knack of knocking? After an hour the place is beginning to have a bad feel so I decide to head on out. Things can only improve – can't they? After just a few miles an American Legion club appears, set in acres of land and with several cars in the car park. This is an alternative and untested approach but anything is better than another batch of rejections at the front doors of private homes. Ignoring the *'Members Only'* sign, I follow the passage through to a bar. It is the Colonel who approaches.

'My dear' he says, much to my astonishment (*'ma'am'* is the norm) 'you are very welcome to pitch your tent absolutely anywhere on our land that you think is suitable. You'll be very safe as there is plenty of choice amongst the trees behind this building. When you've done so, please be sure and come back. I'd like to buy you a drink and hear more about this adventure.'

When I return the bar is filling up with a few very old couples and plenty of considerably older men, many of whom walk with the aid of either a stick, a Zimmer frame or crutches. Any plan of writing up my diary has to be abandoned due to the several offers of wine, beer and pizza. Being chatted up is a novelty and results in a date for breakfast tomorrow with Leo. Will I be stood up? Indeed not. He collects me at eight o'clock and drives to a diner in town. Leo was in England during the war and is living in a time warp, judging from his dogmatic and prejudiced observations. However, he acts in true gentlemanly fashion and does not allow his disabilities and age to prevent him from flirting. Altogether a very unusual breakfast.

There is a skinny island which runs the length of northern Florida and the road through it is not a major highway so it makes for excellent cycling. In places such as Daytona, the Torquay of these parts, every building along the front is a hotel. And just how many variations on names such as *'sea'*, *'beach'*, *'view'*, *'palm'*, *'sand'*, *'coral'* can there be? A few alternatives adding a foreign nuance such as *'vista'*, *'aqua'* and *'del mare'* are amongst them but my favourites are completely irrelevant: *'Ivanhoe'* and *'Robin Hood'*. At least these names would ensure that the guests won't check into the wrong *'view'* – *'Now, darling, what exactly is the name of the hotel we have made our reservation? Is it Ocean View, Sea View, Heavenly View, Lousy View or No View?'*

On the outskirts are the gated communities. Contained within foreboding fences, hundreds of acres of houses are protected by a guarded entrance usually with a barrier. Forbidden territory for a cycling migrant searching for a spot to pitch a tent, no matter how cute the English accent. There are also the condominiums – the human battery cages – usually three storeys, single room width, no yard and restricted parking. Definitely no point knocking on these doors. An eye catching advertising board describes one such place as *'Condomiums For Active Retired'*.

Everyone has recommended, indeed insisted, that St Augustina should be on my list to sightsee as it is *'the oldest city in the States'*. I somehow doubt the truth of the statement, but nevertheless it strikes me as a reasonable option, particularly with a hostel in the town. No random search for one night seems a good enough reason to make the detour. But, I haven't bargained on the fact that it is the New Year weekend with the result that not only is the hostel full, so is the town. Every building in the centre has ceased to be a home or office, converted instead into either a souvenir shop or eating establishment, all succeeding in extracting money from throngs of tourists. There are people and cars everywhere. And to complete my misery, the streets are cobbled – a cyclist's biggest nightmare. There is a compensation as I am able to spend an invaluable couple of hours at the library connected up to my email messages.

Tonight gives a balance to all my astonishing good luck to date, something to focus the mind on never taking anything for granted. The town is a satellite for Jacksonville and consists of endless miles of shopping malls and gated communities. It is five o'clock by the time I come across the only road of normal houses and I am already in a panic. The worst possible scenario then unfolds.

Steve answers the door and spends ten minutes explaining why he cannot let me camp – something to do with grounded teenagers and barking dogs. How he made this last ten minutes is indeed a credit to his guilty conscience. A simple 'no' would have been so much more kind and honest – and quick. He then refers me to a neighbour several doors away named Pam – I am great believer in omens and this feels like a good one. It takes five minutes to attract her attention above the noise of the stereo. Normally I wouldn't have bothered, but he has convinced me she will be delighted to let me stay. She invites me in without hesitation, gives me iced water (just what is needed when both hands and feet are already aching with cold) and interrogates me about how I happen to be standing on her doorstep. (Steve would definitely be hearing from her in the not too distant future.)

After this cross-examination she then informs me 'I don't feel comfortable having you stay over in my yard. This is not about me – it's about my kids. It doesn't seem like a good idea'. (What on earth can she mean by that?)

By now I am feeling very irritated. More than half an hour has been wasted and it's almost dark outside, temperatures sub-zero.

Under the guise of appearing incredibly helpful, she then gives a twenty minute master class in passing the buck that Steve has handed her. She tries to get hold of the school deputy 'who *might* have some ideas', a local friend 'who *might* have two empty condos where you *might* be able to sleep', a church 'who *might* take in people when the temperature drops below 15°C', a local house for battered wives 'where you *might* be able to stay'. (In the case of the last two possibilities she knows neither the name of the contact nor the address, never mind the phone number).

Steve has insisted that I must return to him if Pam can't help – so I do. It then becomes obvious that he only said this because he was confident he would never see me again. He spends another ten minutes repeating the earlier excuses, but this time holding his head in his hand – the pose of someone looking for inspiration. (The bubble above saying *'Of all the houses in Ponte Vedra Beach, why did she have to pick mine?'*)

If nothing else I have to admire his creativity. 'I know just the place. The local fire station is real close – just the other side of the main road. There is always someone there and of course they have beds for the guys on night duty. They will let you stay over. I'm sure they'd be delighted to help. But in case they don't, be sure to come back and I'll see what I can do.' Yeah, right....

Common sense tells me that he must be wrong but mounting desperation encourages me to check. The officer in charge points me to the waste ground behind a closed down supermarket which is not an option as it is very public, very exposed and very high profile, and even if it weren't any of these, it is tarmac and as successful as those nails have been, they're definitely not capable of penetrating this surface.

Continuing down the main road with Alchemy's lights casting their first beams, I notice the unexpected shape of a bungalow and my entreaty brings a succinct and positive result. The only words from the young woman who opens the door are 'Yes, your request is a bit strange. I don't know you and you don't know me.' Well, she's not wrong there. She immediately shuts the door and that is the last I see of her. As she has barely given me time to say *'thank you'*, I am tempted knock a second time to give her a hug to make doubly sure she appreciates how indebted I am (perhaps even ask her if she knows Steve and Pam in which case I have a message for them), but she'd probably sling me off the premises.

I experience a unique New Year's eve. Unfavourable winds and fictitious place names result in finding myself beyond the reach of a town before dark so instead I stop in the middle of nowhere. The tent is snug amongst some trees at the edge of a large wood and having eaten and written up my diary I am in bed by six o'clock. Outside it is already dark and freezing, an ideal time to spend quietly meditating. (What a contrast to the Millennium the previous year on the banks of the Thames, barely able to breath because of the crush of millions of people and absolutely unable to move.) To ensure the cold doesn't penetrate, I am wearing every item of clothing in my luggage, adapting one of the thermal tops in to temporary leggings. The sleeves offer an extra layer of warmth to each leg which makes going to the loo in the middle of the night a challenging manoeuvre. The cold is confirmed in the morning when I take the nails out of the ground. Instead of collapsing, the tent remains upright – the condensation inside has frozen!

During the previous day I had come across two brothers cycling to California. They recommended a hostel which was guaranteed not to be full and $15 would get me supper and a bed for the night. This is my destination today. The place is tucked away deep in the woods, a mile of tortuous muddy craters. It is immediately obvious that this is a New Age creation with more consideration for the environment than for the guests. The two main buildings are geodesic and constructed out of wood. All other rooms are built high on stilts and scattered amongst the trees. The toilets are compost and the water in the shower and basins is liquid ice.

216

It is midday and dozens of bodies wrapped in blankets are asleep on the ground around a huge bonfire, with many more comatose in sleeping bags in one of the domes – signs of a dedicated and thorough celebration of the New Year. Those who are up are wandering, in the true sense of the word, in very alternate clothes – sarongs and sandals (with frost still on the ground). I feel as if I have travelled to another planet. I am the only person older than thirty five and without dreadlocks. While I am absorbing my surroundings, Jessica takes pity on me by giving me rosehip tea served in a jam jar.

'I've been coming here for the past ten years and couldn't imagine spending New Year's Eve anywhere else. It's just wonderful. You always meet up with old friends and make lots of new ones.'

'How far have you driven?' I ask.

'It's about eight hundred miles to get here' she tells me, as if this is not really worth commenting on. I am to discover that this is nothing unusual. Many others have travelled well over a thousand miles – one way.

While we were waiting for the kettle to boil I had spotted the large remaining slice of a delicious chocolate cake and my upbringing overcame all natural instincts to devour it, so I drooled longingly to myself. Some while later I am sitting inside one of the domes (wearing fleece, hat, scarf and gloves as the wood burning stove is not burning wood) when a chap is carried in, apparently unconscious. But no, he has eaten that piece of cake. It wasn't chocolate – it was a marijuana cake and he remains out of it for the rest of the day! I am beginning to think that I was more at home amongst the American Legionnaires, but I've paid my money and there is the supper and a bedroom to look forward to.

Word gets around that a sweat lodge is being set up which is an unexpected and brilliant bonus for me. As the first day of 2001 this will be a very symbolic beginning to the year. Tragically, it is anything but a spiritual experience. It is a complete disaster due to the sub zero temperatures, naïve preparation and the inane outpourings of a couple of the participants.

The supper can be described in the same terms. After a lengthy grace, fifty five individuals holding hands in a large circle are invited to introduce themselves and elaborate their reasons for being here. Perhaps a good idea in the summer with cheese and salad on the menu but with twenty degrees of frost and the warm food being subject to flash freezing, the ritual seems unnecessarily drawn out – it lasts thirty five minutes. There are fifty two people ahead of me in the queue for food and by the time I reach the bowls of rice and stir fry vegetables, every last morsel has gone. And there I was worrying about it not being hot.

And so to bed. The choice is sleep in one of the domes amongst the sarongs and dreadlocks hoping that collective body heat would ensure a degree of warmth, or go for a room on my own in a tree house with the risk of being frozen solid by the morning. The rooms have very thin wooden walls on three sides and wire anti-mosquito netting on the fourth. Insulation factor – nil, and the temperature registers 15°F. The mattress is covered with black heavy gauge plastic which guarantees that any warmth remaining in your body is sucked out. The tent would definitely have been a warmer option but by now it is too late. For an insane moment I seriously consider wrapping it around me as an extra layer of insulation.

This alternate hostel has definitely delivered alternate value for $15. A unique lifetime experience, but as I lie awake shivering through a long, dark night, somehow warm food (well any food) plus a warm bed feels preferable.

My departure at dawn goes unnoticed. My return to normality is marked a couple of hours later when I stop for breakfast and Eleanor and her husband ask if they can join me. They have made the connection with Alchemy which is locked up outside and want to hear my story. An hour passes and thoroughly warmed through with wonderful food and steaming coffee, I disappear to the loo and on my return discover that Eleanor has paid for my breakfast.

Chapter Twenty Seven

It is the final day on the road. My cycling limit is reached amidst the sprawling suburbia outside Savannah and I make an intuitive spontaneous choice to cross the busy dual carriageway and weave through the shops to the houses beyond. The first doorstep I choose is opened by Jowanna. A widow, living with her ninety year old mother, she tells me that five years ago a Finnish cyclist had pitched his tent in her back yard and she would be more than happy for me to do the same. She has a visitor and will speak to me later. I have set everything up, including the twenty articles of clothing to be worn when the sun drops (twenty degrees of frost is forecast) when Jowanna reappears, tells me to pack everything up and join her and her mother. After the delicious home cooked food, she invites one her sons and his wife over to meet me. They are both members of the local police and are due to go to Bosnia, which is causing Jowanna deep concerns.

When I leave in the morning my Achilles tendon gives me grief during the fifteen mile ride into town. It has been graunching increasingly during the last few days – the only physical discomfort of the journey other than that inflicted by the savage saddle – and I decide to cover the final stage by bus. Having failed to travel around the States in my early twenties, it will be an opportunity to experience the infamous Greyhound bus.

After an idyllic couple of hours riding round the beautiful old town of Savannah, I return to the Visitors Welcome Centre. (I called in originally to collect information and was emphatically warned about the dangers of cycling around the city!) The warmth and comfort of the place is ideal for writing the last batch of postcards and the restaurant area is crowded. A couple with two very young children approach me, realising that the bicycle outside must belong to me. Before starting a family, they had cycled from Italy to Sweden and they are very keen to hear my story, so much so that they return in the early evening to take me out for dinner. This *'last supper'* seems to symbolise the journey. I was expecting to spend several hours on my own at the bus station waiting for the late departure of a bus to Charlotte. Instead a family of strangers show spontaneous generosity and kindness, keen to share my experience and treat me to a memorable and delicious meal.

But I still have to get to Charlotte by bus.

The very word *'Greyhound'* conjures up romantic long distance journeys. How wrong, how very wrong – long distance, maybe; but romantic? The first unwelcome discovery is that company policy insists that bicycles have to be boxed. This is utterly preposterous but Job's Worth is impervious to my arguments and entreaties. The box is provided, or more accurately sold for $15 and a further $10 is charged to load it. (All other parcels or extra large cases which have to be stored in the compartments underneath travel free, which adds to my sense of rage and injustice.) And because the box is barely large enough for a child's bike, Alchemy has to be dismantled. It is during this process that a male human sledge hammer intervenes and insists on taking over, in spite of my reassurance that I can manage.

Amidst the most revolting coughing, sniffing, spluttering and sneezing, this maniac repeats fifty times 'I'm only tryin' to help, ma'am' and I am very wary about telling him to go away.

The bicycle is subjected to violent treatment as he tries to force it into the box.

'Please – really – this isn't working – I can manage – it's very kind of you but – I've done this before....' I say, desperately trying to regain control.

'I'm only tryin' to help, ma'am.'

He finally grabs the parcel tape to seal the bulging box, pedals and handlebars protruding, which makes even more of a farce of the whole proceedings, and succeeds, because of utter ineptitude, in slicing his finger on my precious Swiss army knife. Having handed the partially packed bike over to the Greyhound luggage section, I sit down shaking with relief and rage, when this vile man sits alongside, sniffing, coughing, spluttering, sneezing and now bleeding all over me. Is the local asylum short of a lunatic?

'I'm a taxi driver, ma'am. Anything you want to know, just ask. There's no need to worry about the cut. It's nothing. I had a very bad car crash and ended up with thirty staples in my head.'

It's a pity they didn't spare a few for his mouth.

He is surrounded by several enormous shopping bags which appear to be his only luggage and proceeds to show me the contents. They are toys – the sort that one sees in the shops and wonders just who on earth buys them. This is the guy. Huge battery operated cheap plastic gadgets, all bought for his mother, and amongst them a frog, a duck and a toilet. Not only do they move (including the toilet) but they talk and sing (their IQ undoubtedly higher than his).

'Listen to the words, ma'am.' 'Look at his eyes, ma'am.' 'Watch the seat, ma'am.'

Oblivious to body language (I am by now all but falling off the end of the seat, arms folded and back towards him), he continues to enthuse all over me. The bus cannot arrive a second too soon.

When it does, it is ancient and dilapidated. There is no toilet, no air conditioning, no music, no video, no facilities for hot or cold drinks and no seat reservation system – all of which were accepted standards and policy in Turkey. At $85 it is also very expensive and the local asylum is surely now empty as it would appear that majority of the passengers have also escaped from it.

During the journey there is an outbreak of fisticuffs over seat preferences and the driver has to act as referee. There is violent and lengthy argument about the use of a reading light. A woman throws a fit, her hand luggage ending up scattered on the floor amongst passengers' feet. A child who cannot get comfortable enough to sleep ensures that nobody else does by complaining loudly and incessantly to her mother. A man carrying his luggage in flimsy plastic bags loses the entire contents and chaos ensues as he tries to rectify the situation. Apart from intolerable and inconsiderate behaviour, the other qualification for passengers appears to be a weight of not less than twenty stone.

My good luck holds as my neighbour qualifies as the only other sane person on board. A tiny grandmother who has spent several weeks with her family over Christmas and is returning home.

Arriving at the bus station in Charlotte at four o'clock in the morning, it is astonishing to come across such a seething mass of people. Finding a quiet place is not easy and means walking some distance through the terminal. It is at these times that several pairs of arms would be an asset, or at least eyes in the back and sides of the head. It would be cruel to have one of the panniers stolen at this stage. Restoring the violated bicycle is easier than before; perhaps a sign that my mechanical skills are improving. The help this time is restricted to quips and comments from passing cleaners, even a policeman. 'Decided the bus wasn't quick enough, hey, ma'am?' Then it is a matter of sitting it out till daylight before my final leg to Tega Cay.

Robin and Julie, another RSA contact, have generously invited me to stay so it is with them that I sort out the final arrangements for the flight home.

(During my stay, Julie invited me to join a group of her friends for coffee. She introduced me as a friend who had cycled from England. She then went on to list some of the countries – Hungary, Rumania, Bulgaria, Turkey, Pakistan, Thailand, Laos, China – it was obvious that the group were deeply unimpressed, bored and on the point of nodding off. Then Julie said '.... and she crossed over from Mexico into Texas .... ' Before another word escaped her mouth, the group erupted. 'My god, you are telling us that you've cycled all the way here from Texas?' 'Did you say Texas?' 'Good heavens, that's incredible.' 'Texas – are you kidding?' 'Texas – Amazing, I can't believe it.' 'Is that really true? All that way' and 'Whow – which way did you get here?' The rest of the world.... Irrelevant!)

I have created a scenario for one last potential nervous breakdown. With no evidence of arriving in America, what will happen when I leave? My only proof of entry, and how long I have been here, is my diary, so this is packed handily at the top of one of the panniers. When the time comes, the staff at the check in desk are wonderfully helpful. One goes so far as to fudge the necessary immigration form and my usual panic over Alchemy's safety is unnecessary. The airline provide free of charge a box the size of a shed so the bicycle is literally wheeled straight into it and at their suggestion, two panniers are also packed inside, leaving one to be checked in and one as hand luggage. Various earlier phone calls had indicated that the charges for the bicycle and the excess luggage would together amount to more than the cost of my single flight ticket. The flexibility and attitude of the staff results in not needing to hand over a dime.

I arrive back in time for the birth of my second grandchild. Sitting in Russell and Pippa's kitchen drinking tea, it is as if I have never been away. Russell has a map of the world on the wall to help Ella, his four year old daughter, try and understand where I've been. The furthest she has travelled is to Pembrokeshire and Russell has represented my journey in slices of 'London – Pembrokeshire' distances! What a perfect perspective.

They have received all my update emails so there is no need for them to ask 'How did it go.... ?' 'What was the weather like.... ?' 'Was the food good.... ?'

What started off as a bicycle ride developed in to so much more. Alchemy had of course provided the means to move on each day but the entire focus of journey has been about

224

people. Whatever global problems might be, individuals at a local level really want to help. Altruism does exist. And I have discovered that there is such a thing as a free lunch, as well as a free supper and a free breakfast.... and so much more besides.

(And if you're having trouble losing weight....)

Postscript

Just one final word. Having returned from this long journey unharmed and unscathed, the perfect symbolic postscript came just a few weeks later. On the pavement outside my son's home in Wimbledon, I was about to wave goodbye to him and his family. Ready to cycle off I was standing astride the bike when it inexplicably toppled over. With my foot trapped in the pedal, I was dragged over into an embarrassing heap in the gutter.

This incident broke two bones, one in my knee and the other in my foot and I ended up in plaster from ankle to thigh for six weeks.

…. Nobody had warned me about the dangers of cycling in Wimbledon……